BASES FOR TRANSPARENT SPINNERS

For Use in Generating Random Events
for Classroom Games and Activities

Dale Seymour

DALE SEYMOUR PUBLICATIONS

Cover design by Rachel Gage

Copyright © 1987 by Dale Seymour Publications. All rights reserved. Printed in the United States of America. Published simultaneously in Canada.

Limited reproduction permission: The publisher grants permission to individual teachers who have purchased this book to reproduce the blackline masters as needed for use with their own students. Reproduction for an entire school or school district or for commercial use is prohibited.

Order number DS15802
ISBN 0-86651-430-9

Contents

Introduction	v
Undivided Spinner Bases	1
Spinner Bases: Two Sectors	3
Spinner Bases: Three Sectors	8
Spinner Bases: Four Sectors	12
Spinner Bases: Five Sectors	16
Spinner Bases: Six Sectors	20
Spinner Bases: Seven Sectors	25
Spinner Bases: Eight Sectors	29
Spinner Bases: Nine Sectors	33
Spinner Bases: Ten Sectors	37
Circular Protractor	42

Introduction

For many math games and activities, including probability experiments, teachers and students need a simple way to generate random events. One of the most flexible tools for this purpose is the transparent spinner, a device made of clear plastic with a free-spinning metal arrow attached. Such a spinner can be combined with different spinner bases to simulate a wide variety of events. This book of blackline masters offers more than 40 different bases for use with transparent spinners, enabling you to create professional-looking custom spinners for all your class needs.

How to Use This Book

You may copy any of the spinner pages in this book, using either regular copier paper or transparency film (to make spinners for use with an overhead projector). It is recommended that you photocopy directly from the book, rather than remove the pages.

You or your students may use colored felt-tip pens to decorate the spinner bases. To make a more permanent spinner, tape or laminate the desired spinner base onto heavy card stock. For a spinner base that you expect to use frequently, you may find it convenient to tape the transparent spinner to that base.

In the following pages you will find spinner bases with anywhere from two to ten equal sectors. For each basic type, this book provides one numbered base, one lettered base, and one base with different color names in each sector. In addition, one blank example of each type is provided to allow teachers or students to enter their own designations in the sectors.

On pages 1 and 2 you will find undivided circles to use for designing your own spinner bases. Use the circular protractor master on page 42 to create spinner bases with other than 2-10 sectors or with various combinations of unequal sectors.

The masters in this book offer spinner bases in two different sizes. Additional size variations can be created if you have access to a photocopy machine with an enlargement/reduction feature.

Transparent blank spinners for use with these spinner bases are available from numerous educational suppliers, including the publisher of this book. Refer to the current Dale Seymour Publications catalog for ordering information.

TRANSPARENT SPINNER BASES   UNDIVIDED

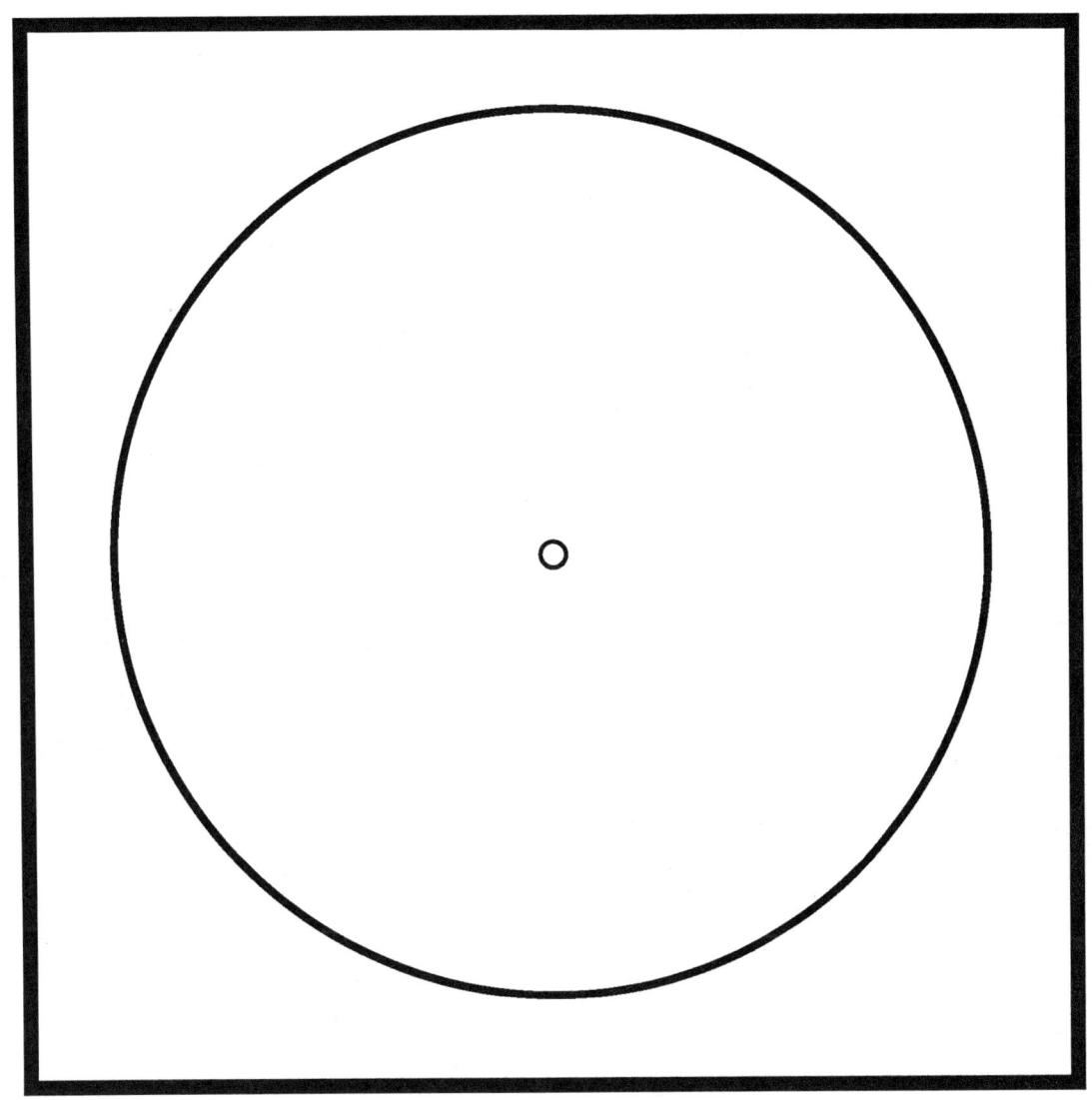

COPYRIGHT © 1987 BY DALE SEYMOUR PUBLICATIONS

TRANSPARENT SPINNER BASES  UNDIVIDED

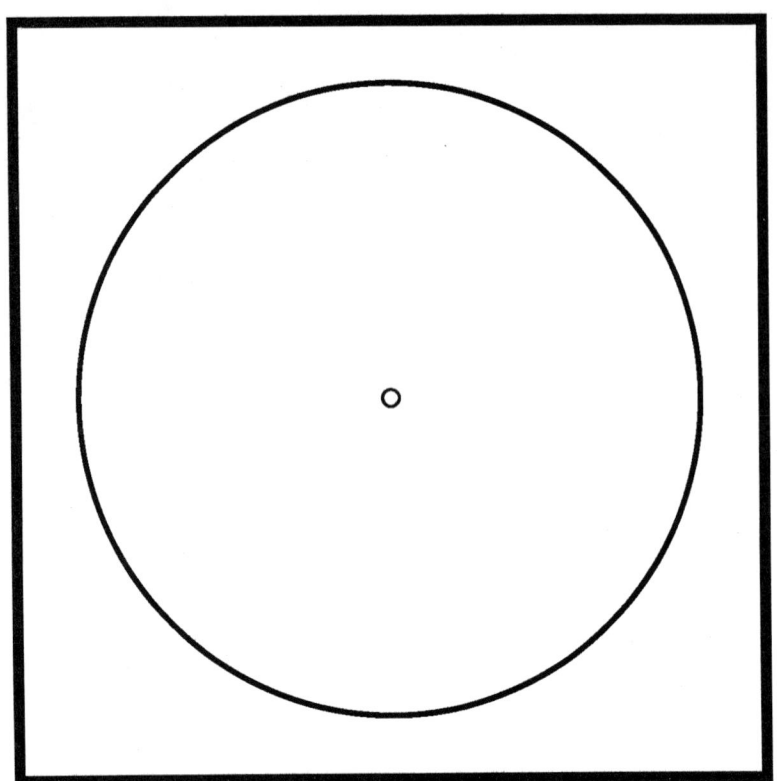

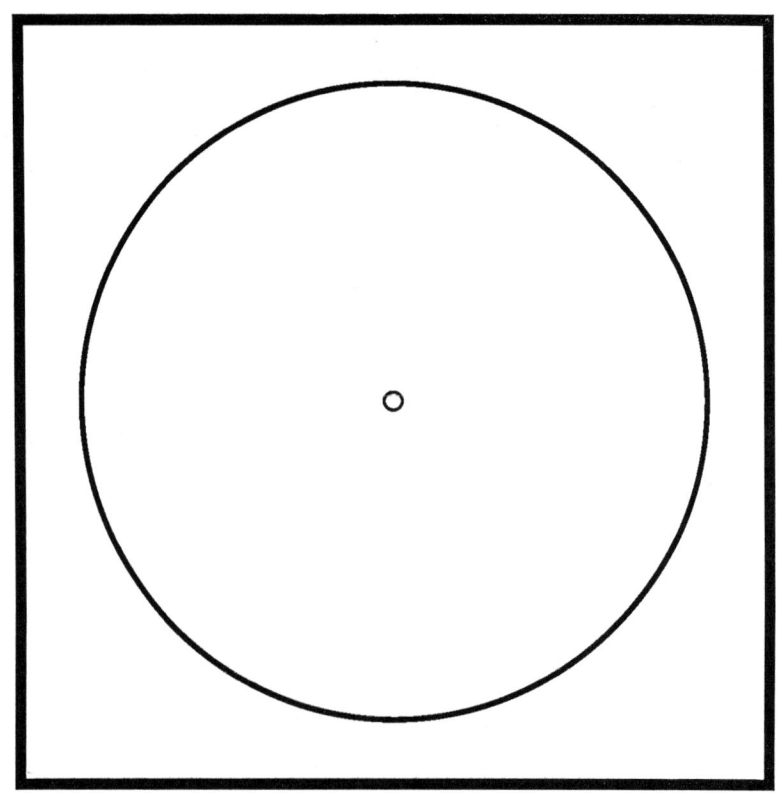

TRANSPARENT SPINNER BASES — TWO SECTORS

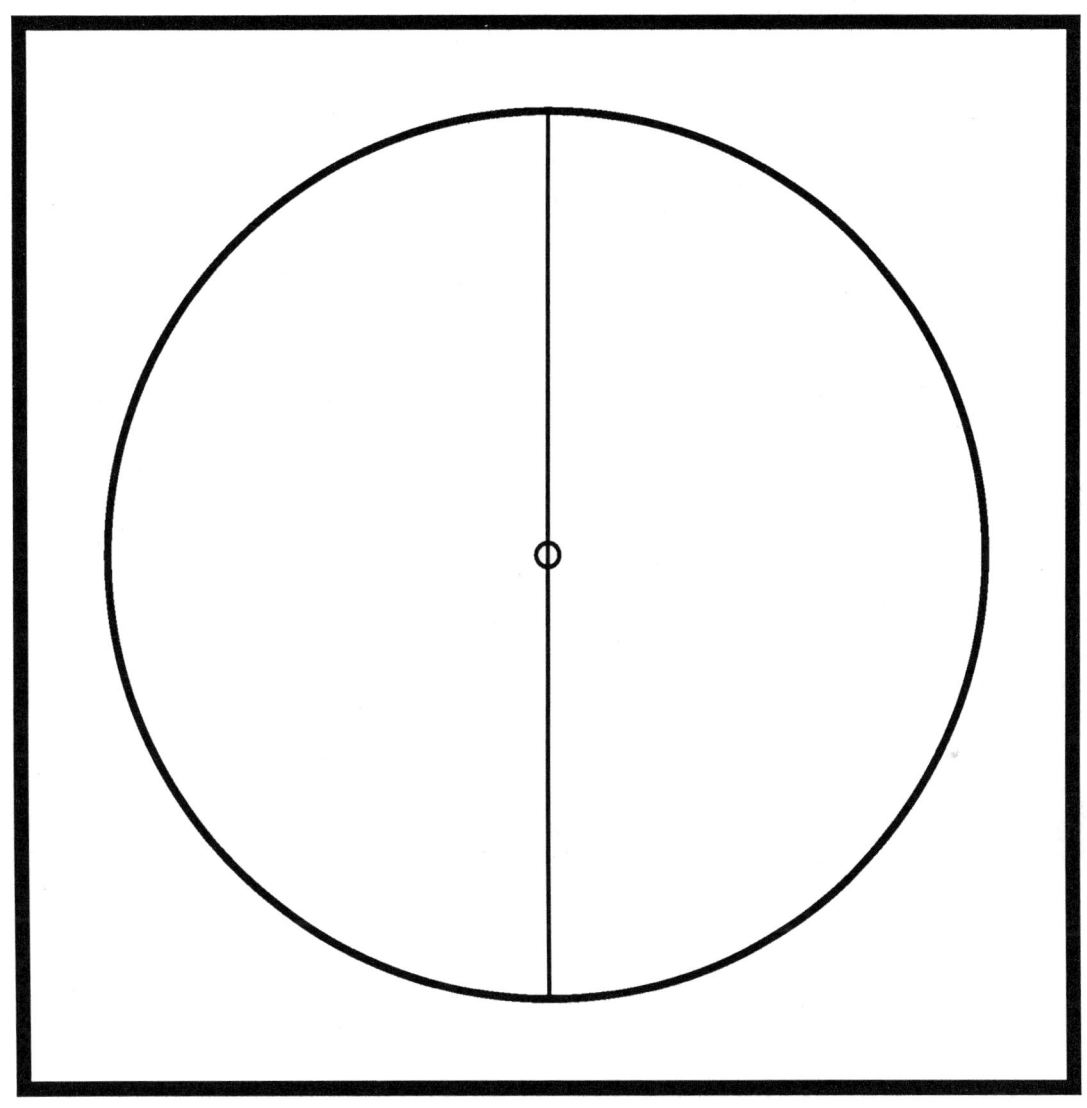

TRANSPARENT SPINNER BASES — TWO SECTORS

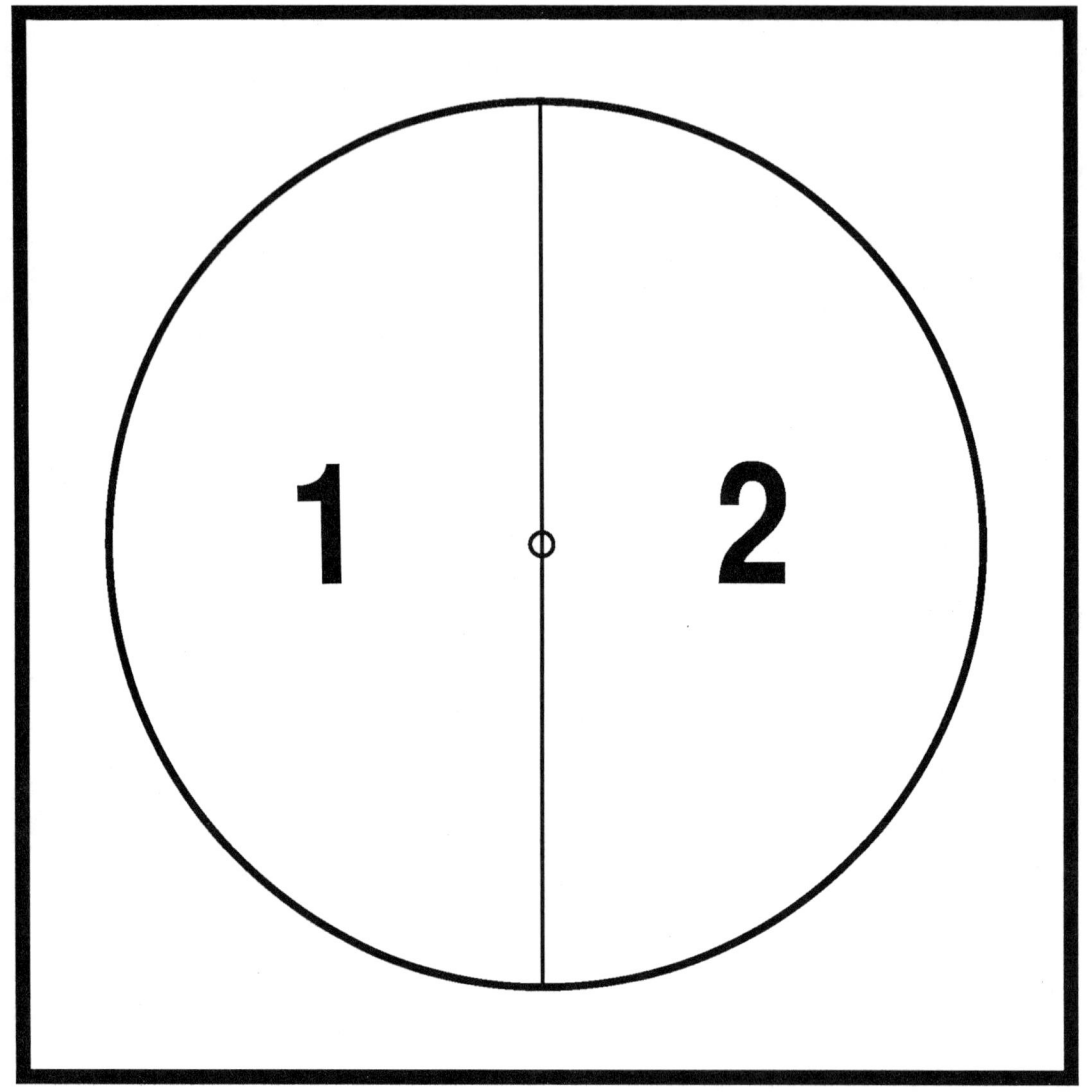

TRANSPARENT SPINNER BASES  TWO SECTORS

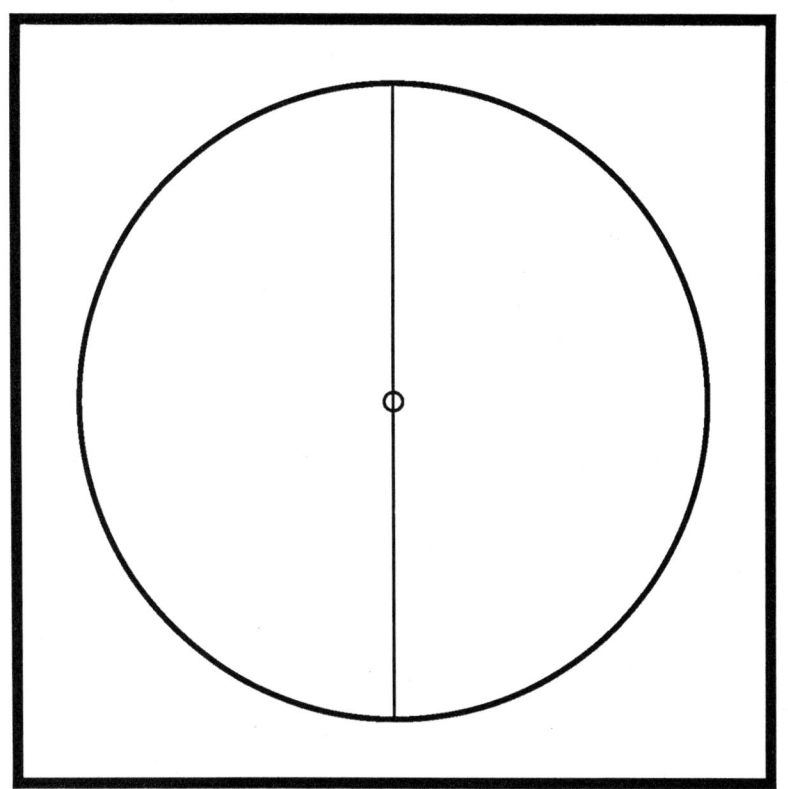

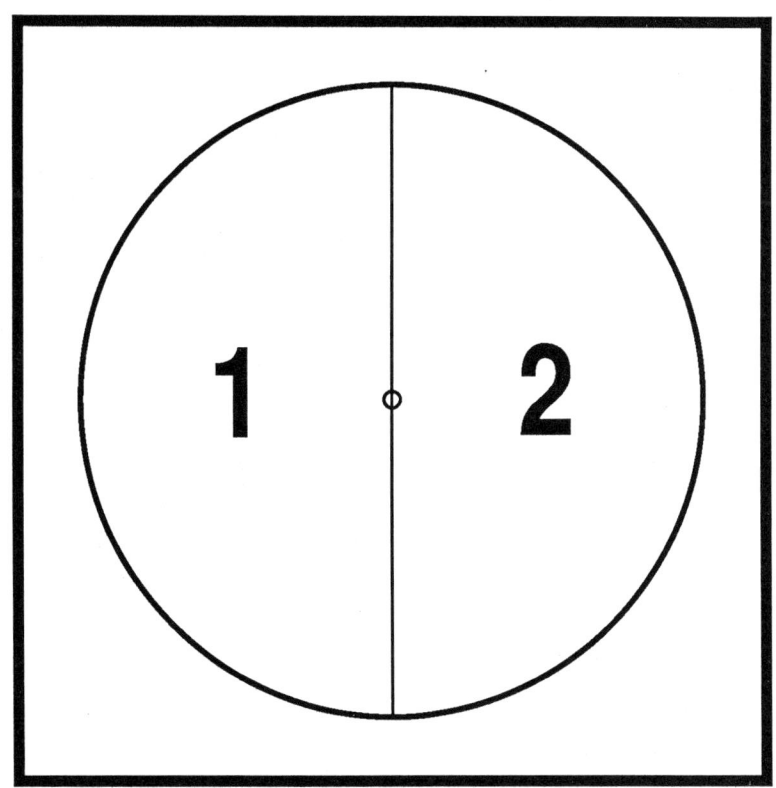

TRANSPARENT SPINNER BASES  TWO SECTORS

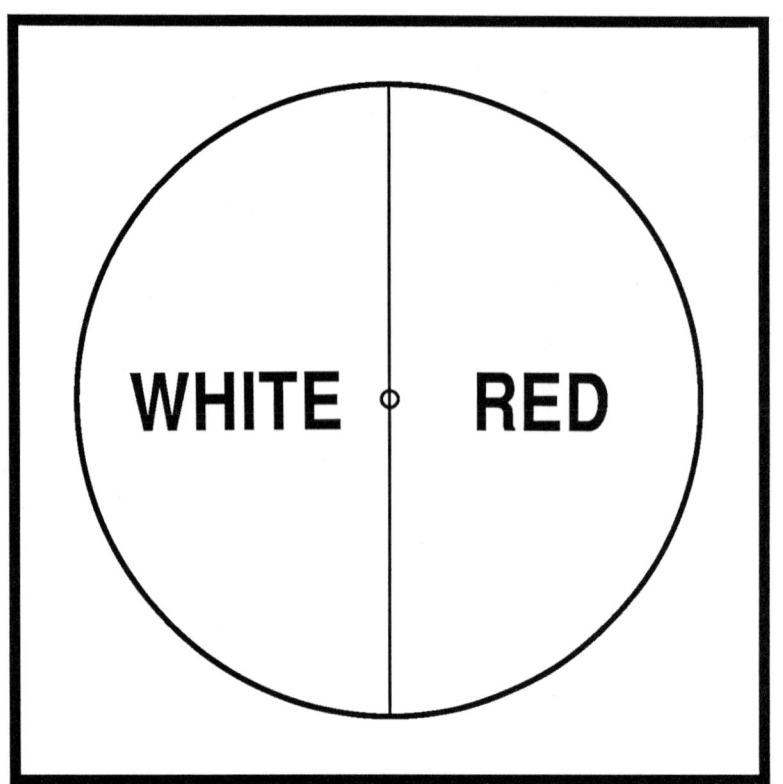

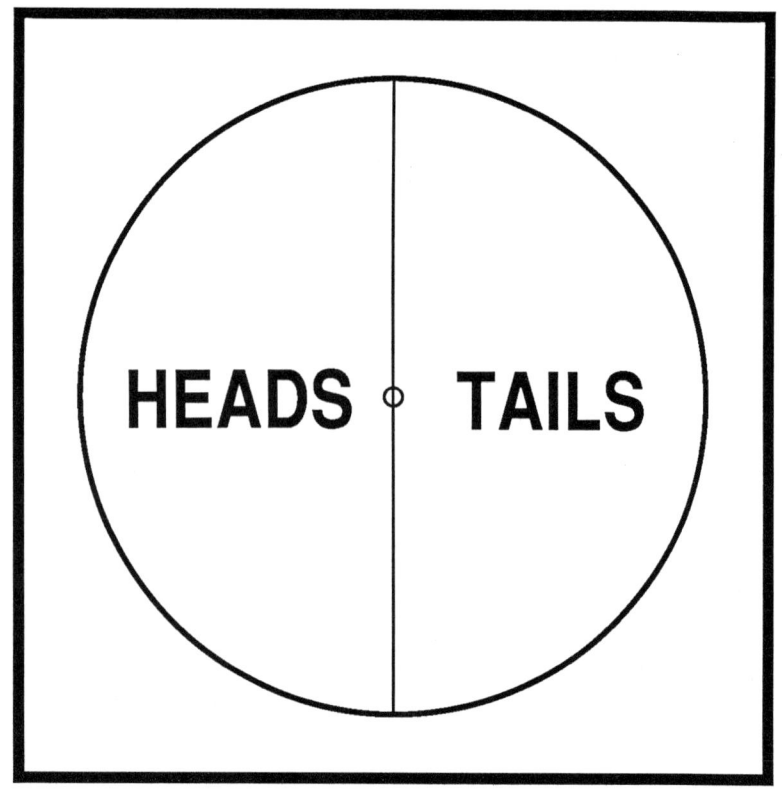

TRANSPARENT SPINNER BASES  TWO SECTORS

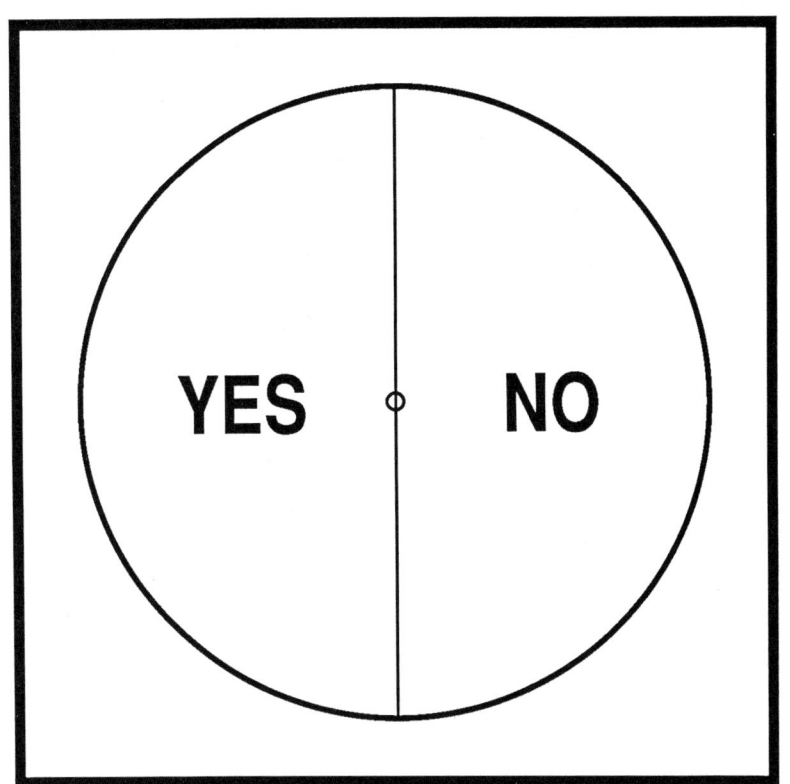

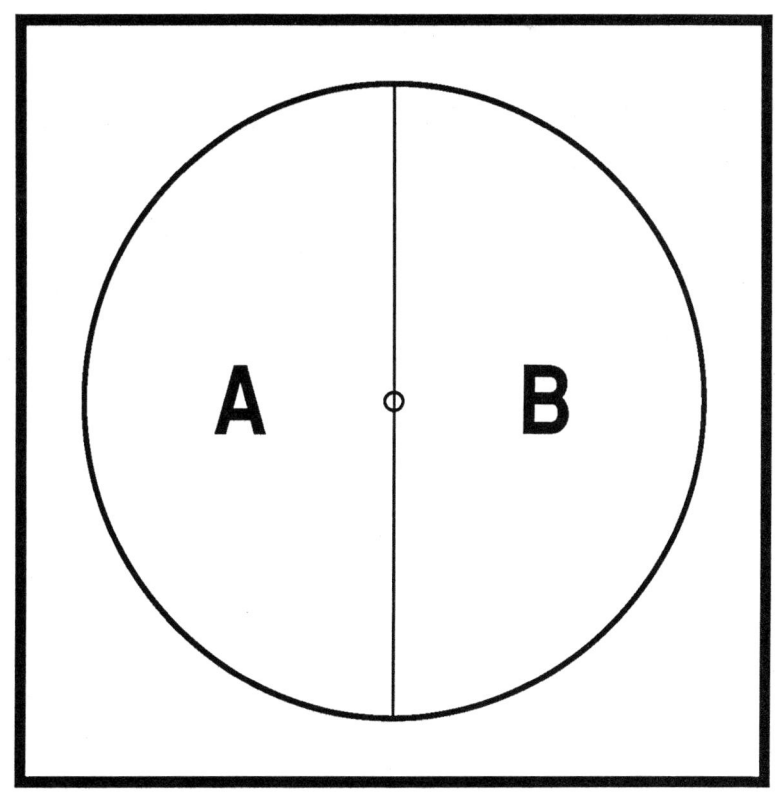

COPYRIGHT © 1987 BY DALE SEYMOUR PUBLICATIONS

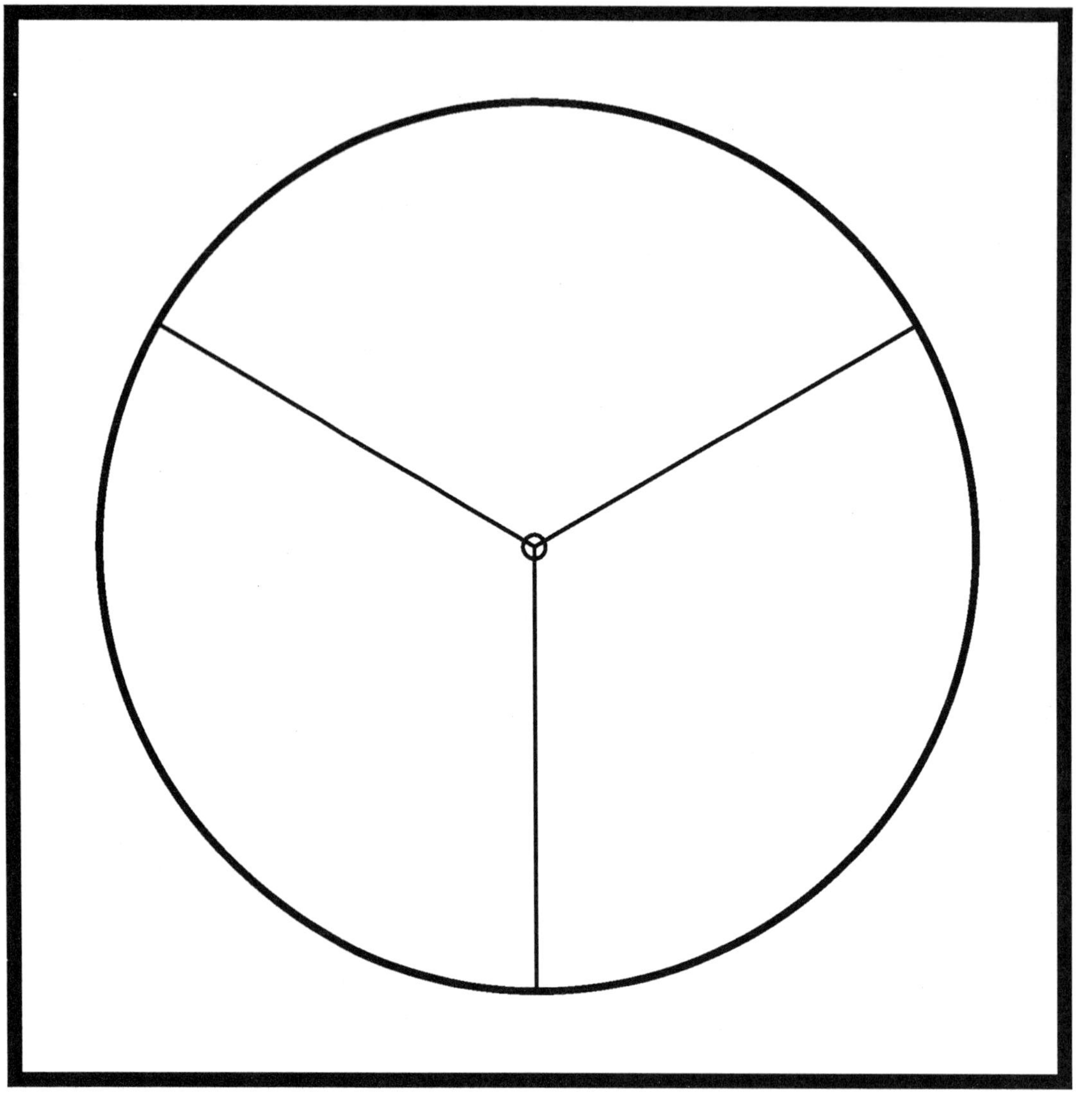

Transparent Spinner Bases  Three Sectors

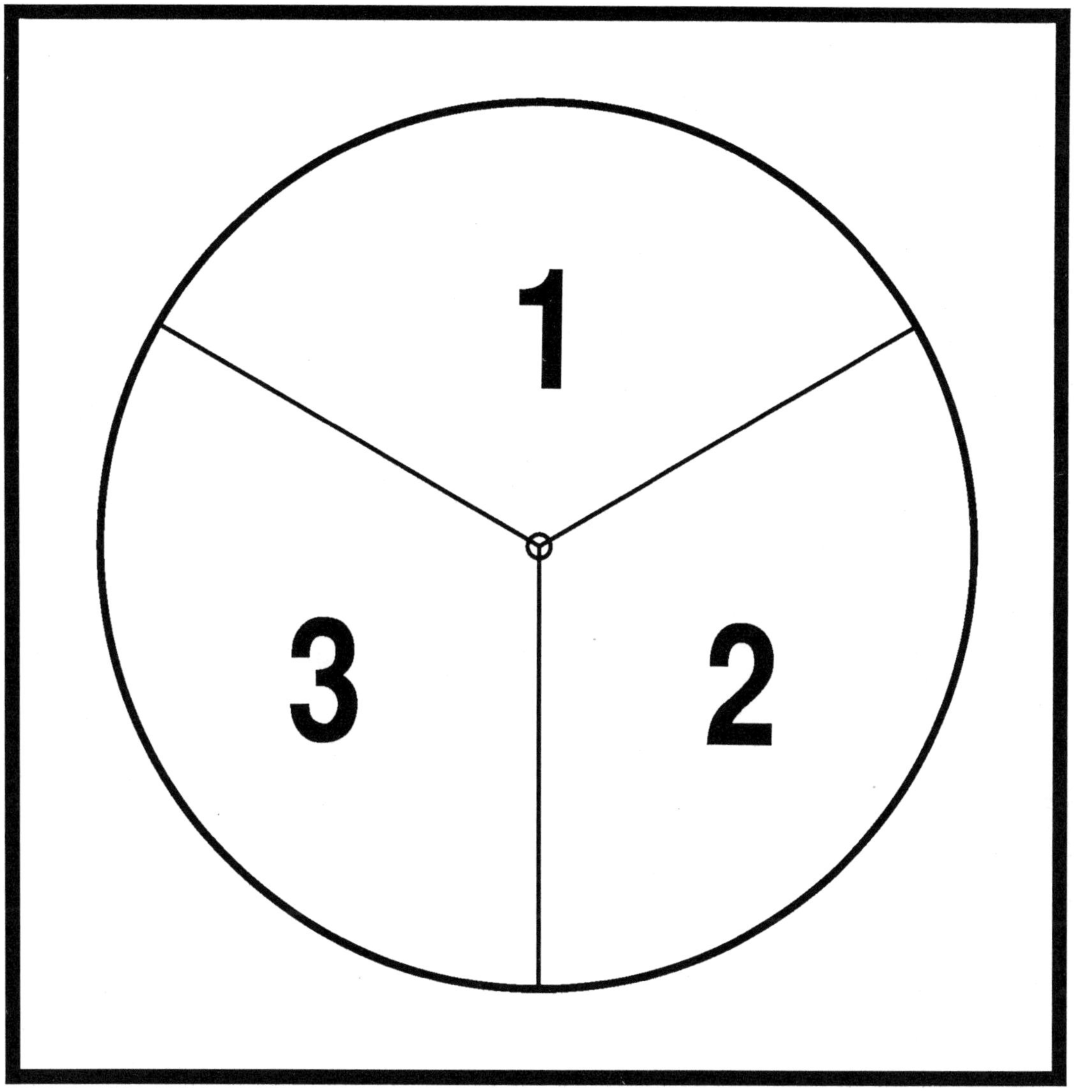

TRANSPARENT SPINNER BASES  THREE SECTORS

TRANSPARENT SPINNER BASES  THREE SECTORS

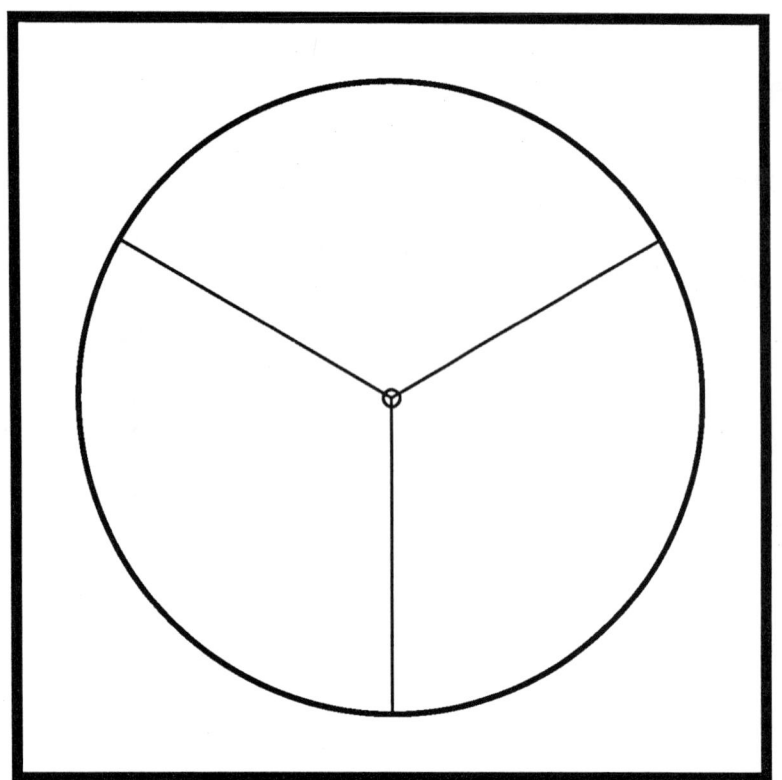

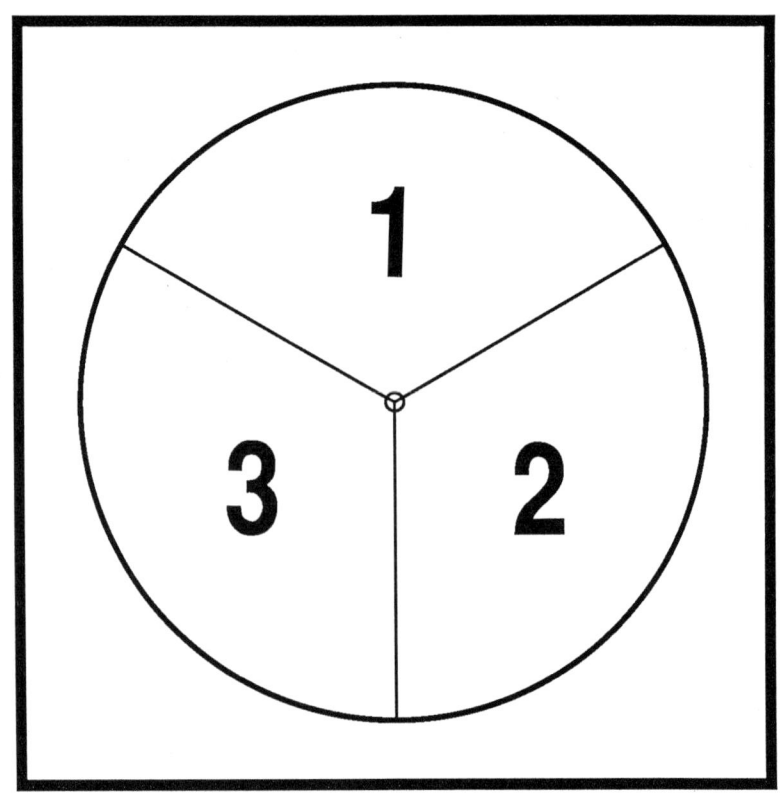

Transparent Spinner Bases  Three Sectors

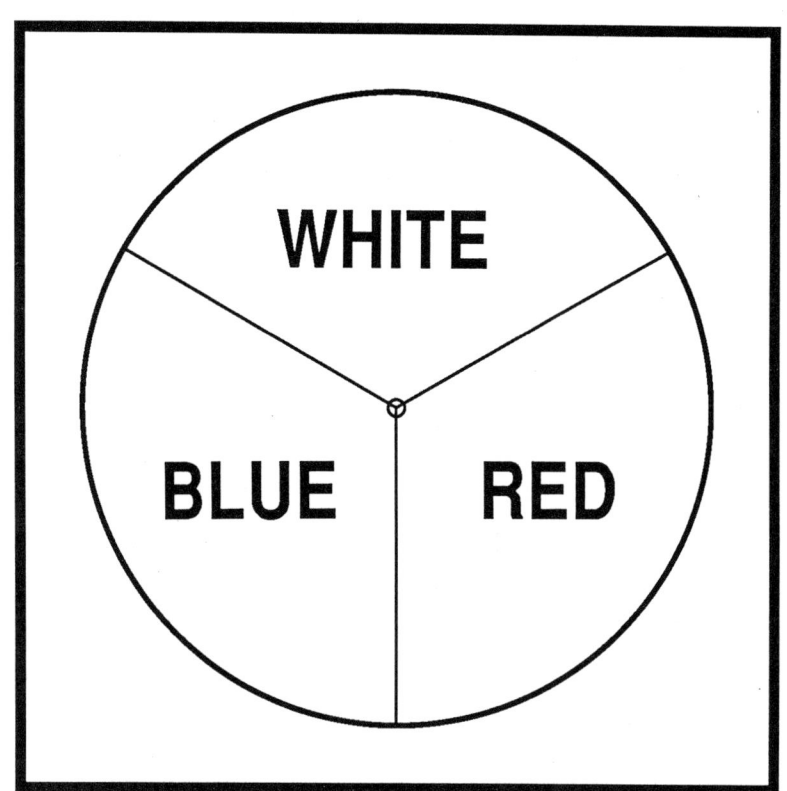

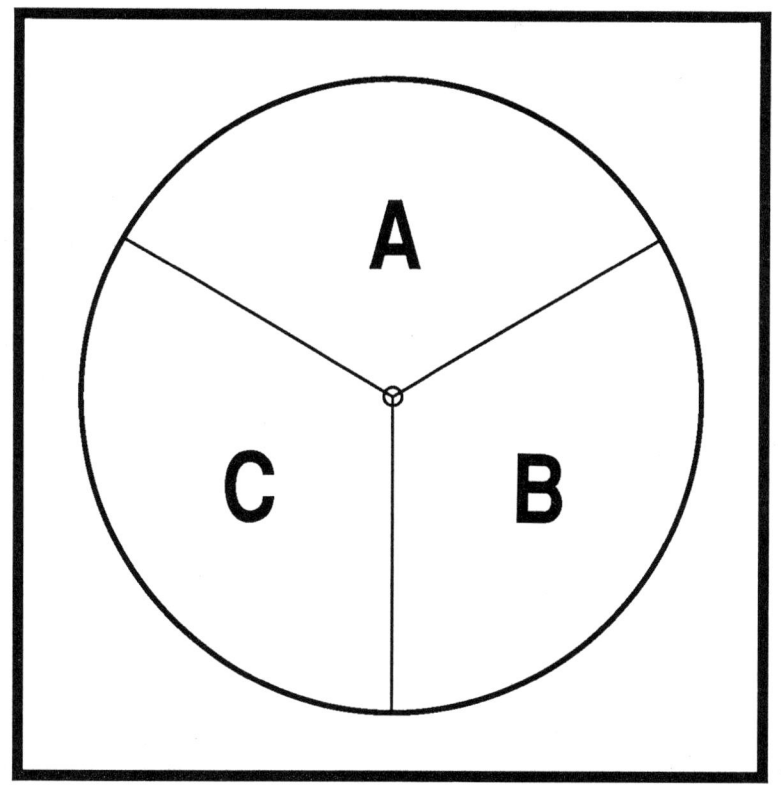

COPYRIGHT © 1987 BY DALE SEYMOUR PUBLICATIONS

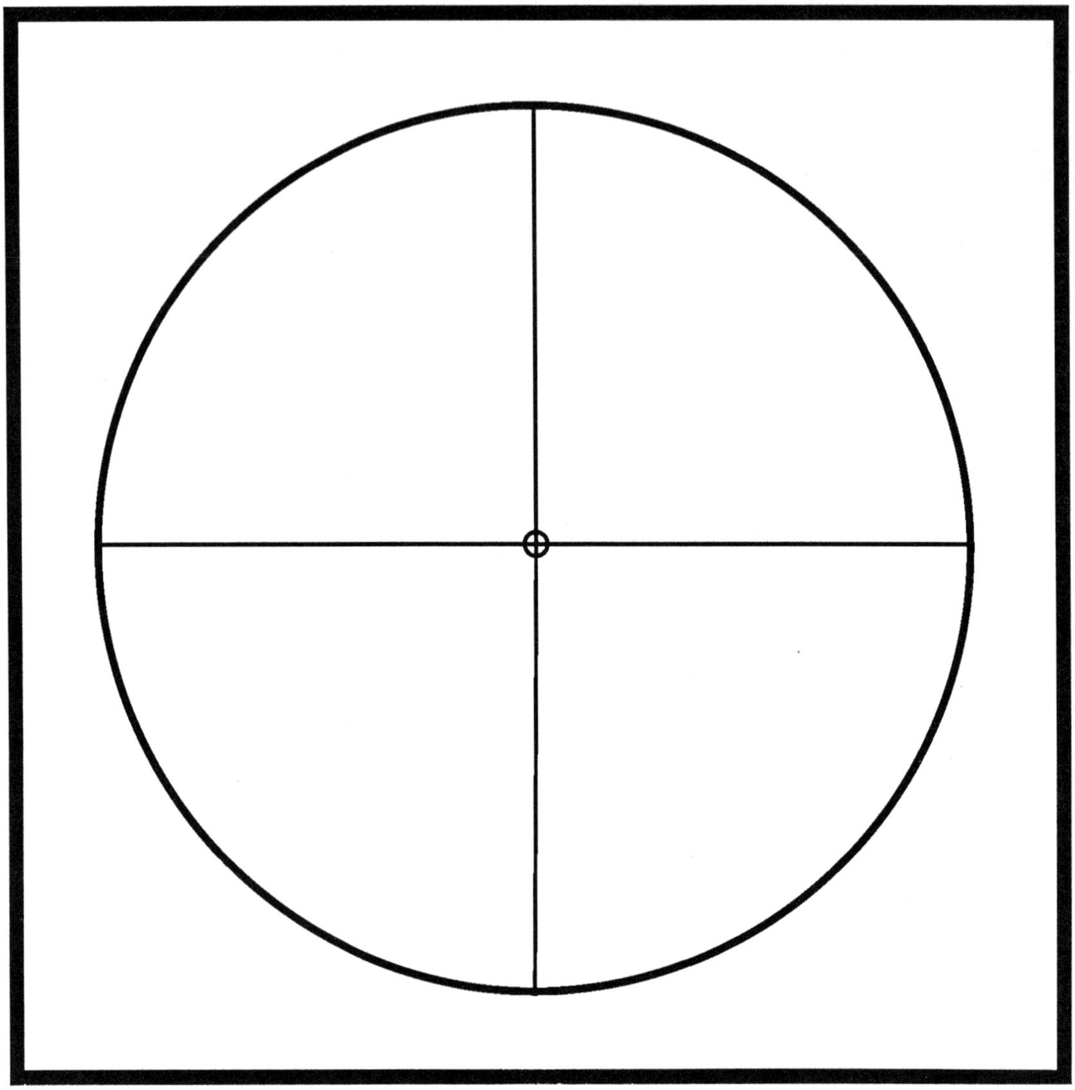

TRANSPARENT SPINNER BASES  FOUR SECTORS

TRANSPARENT SPINNER BASES — FOUR SECTORS

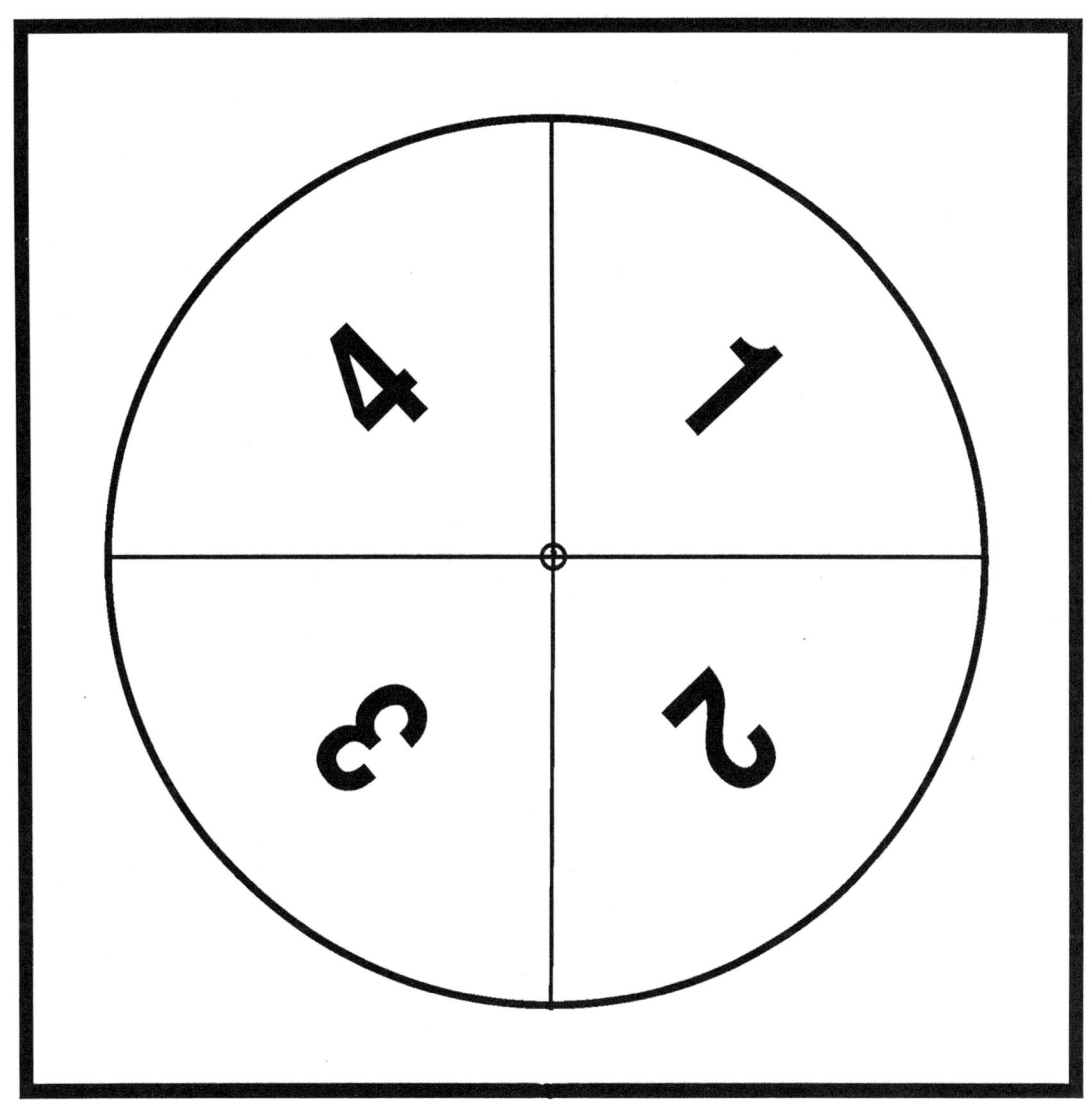

TRANSPARENT SPINNER BASES  FOUR SECTORS

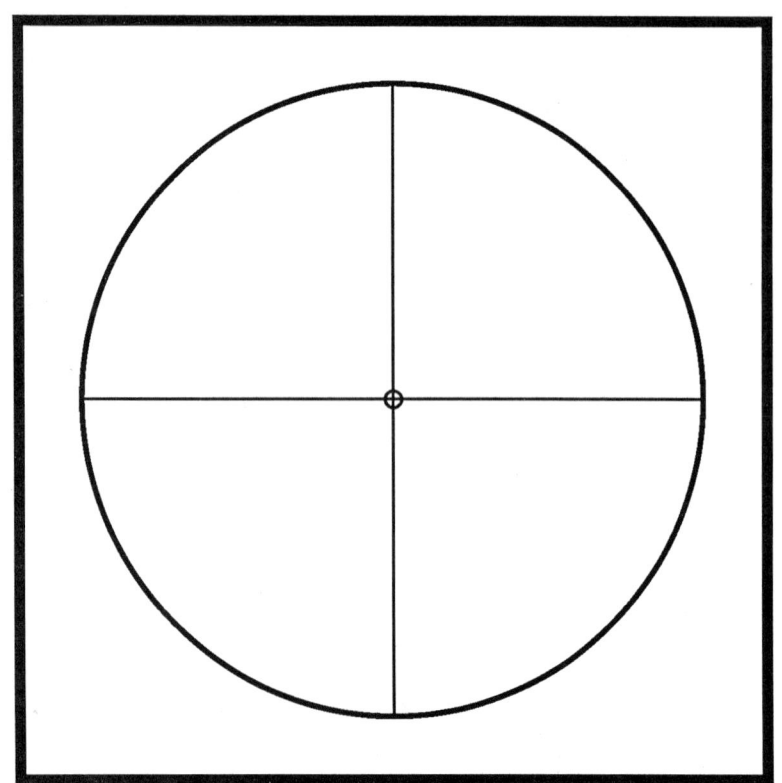

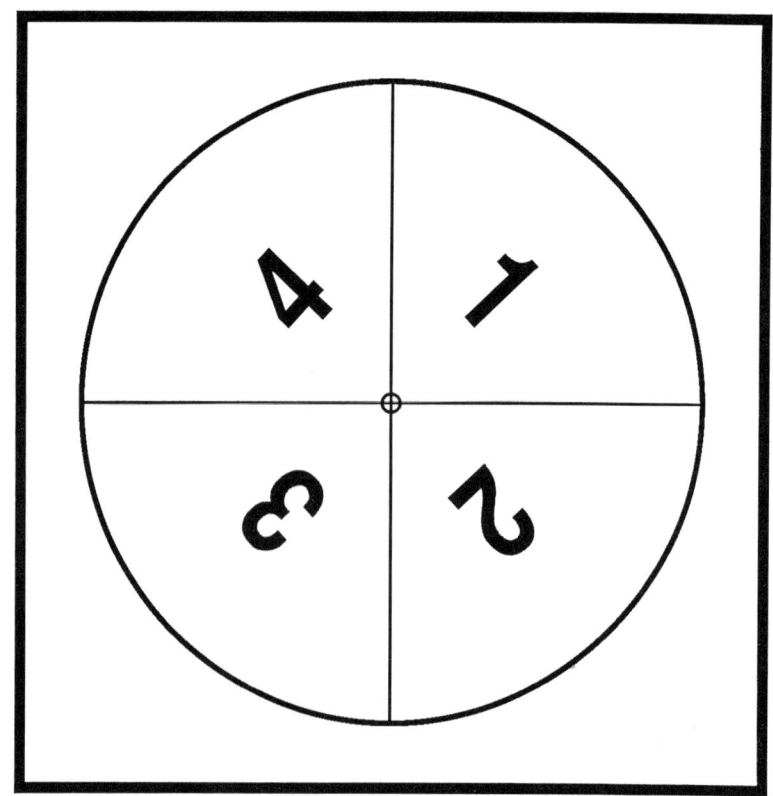

TRANSPARENT SPINNER BASES  FOUR SECTORS

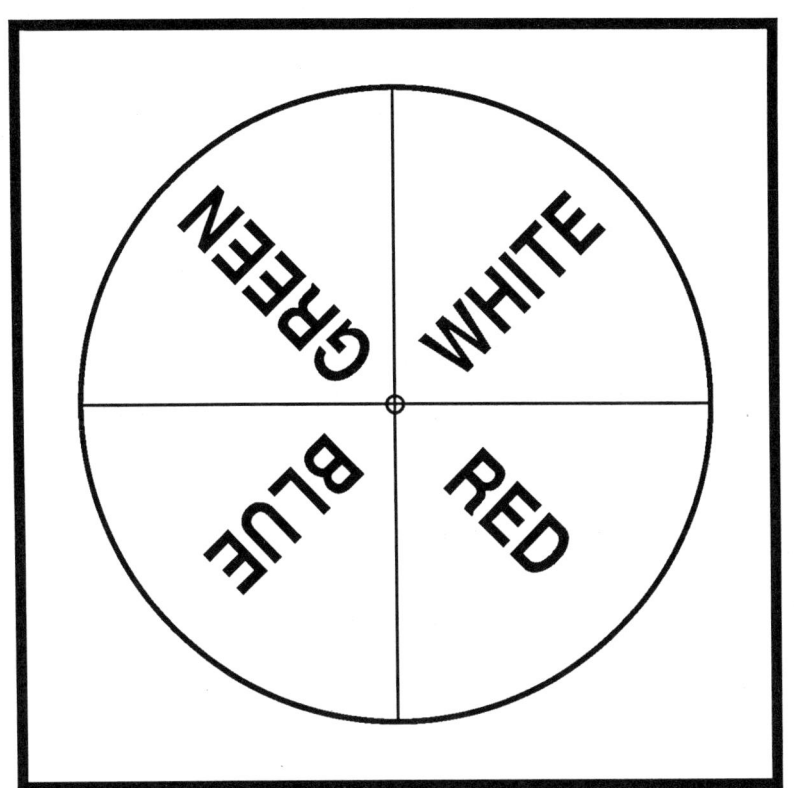

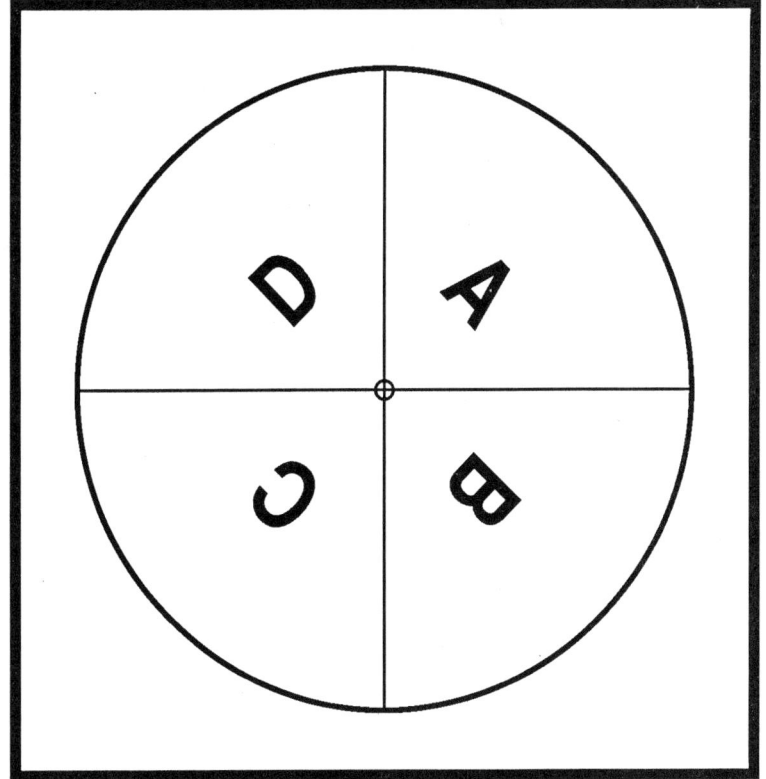

COPYRIGHT © 1987 BY DALE SEYMOUR PUBLICATIONS

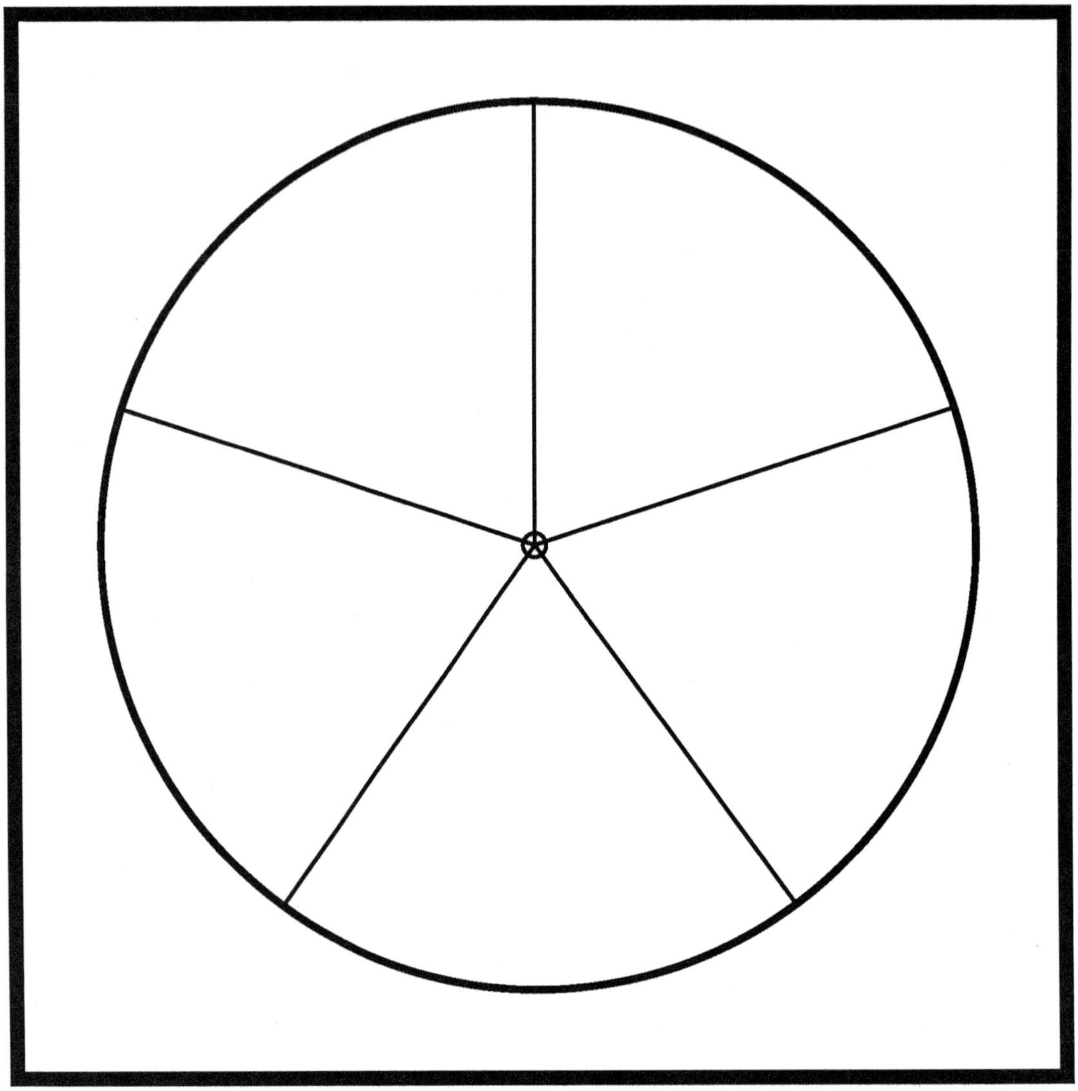

Transparent Spinner Bases  FIVE SECTORS

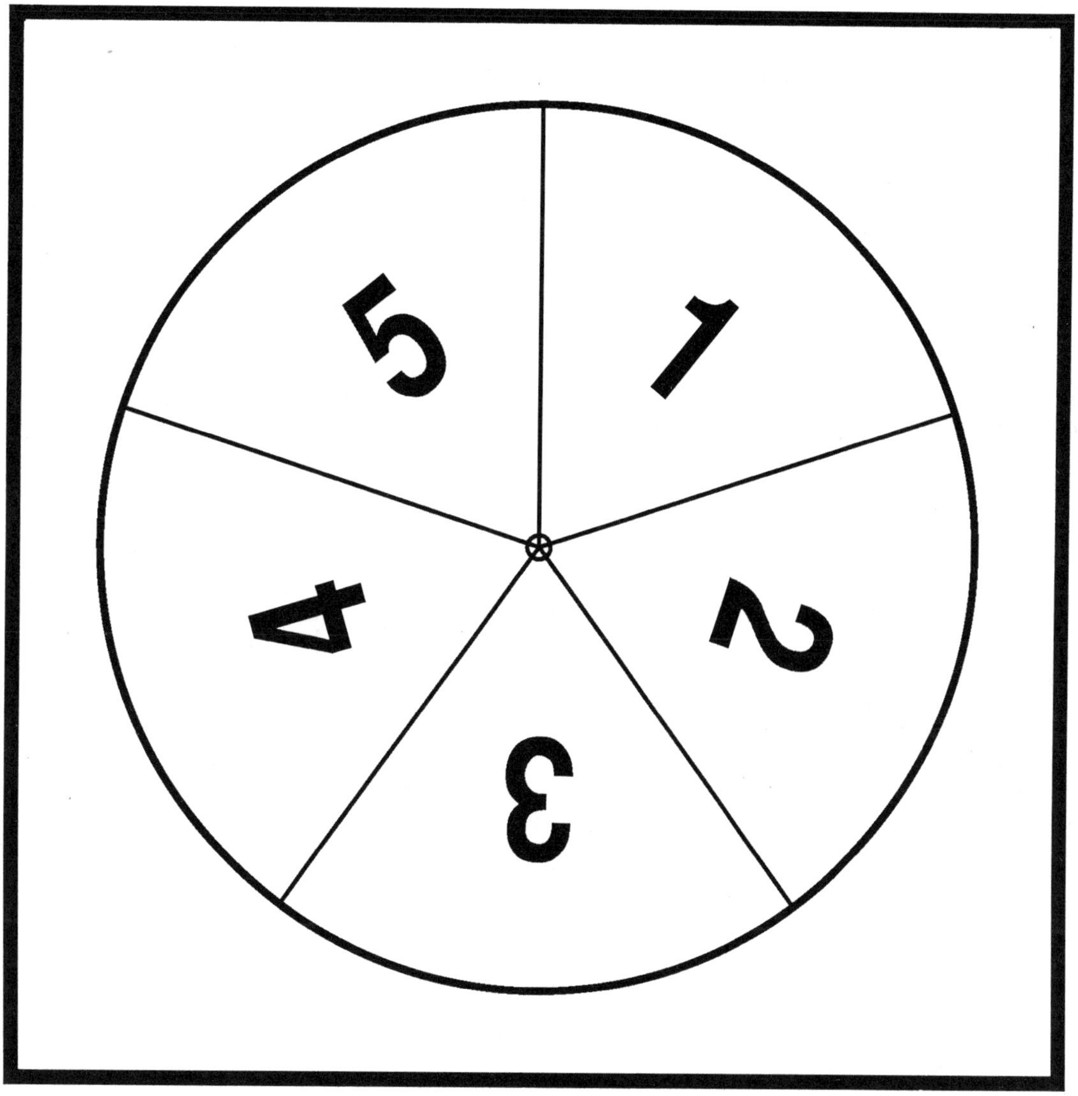

TRANSPARENT SPINNER BASES  FIVE SECTORS

17

Transparent Spinner Bases  Five Sectors

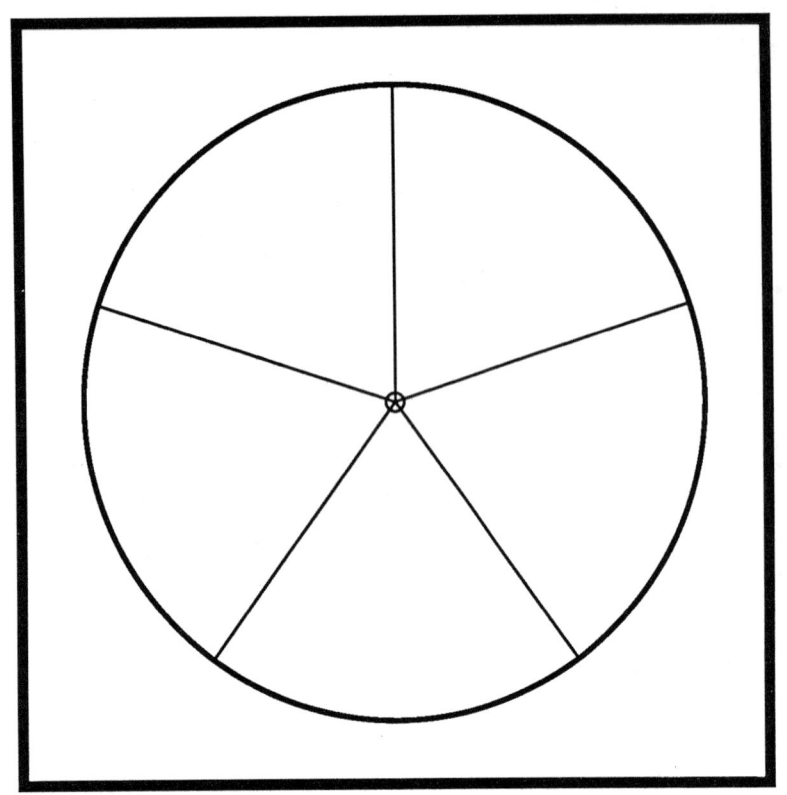

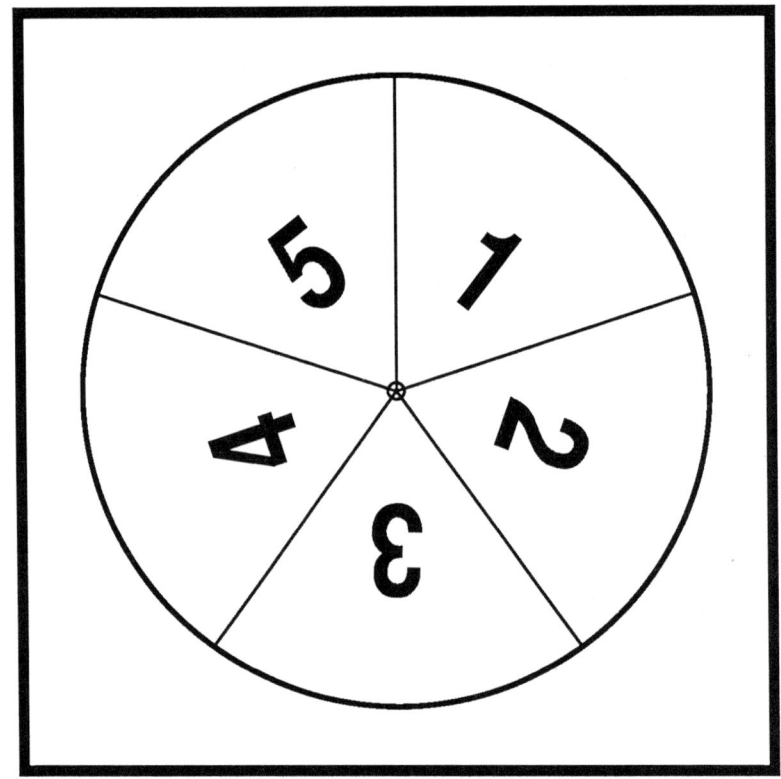

TRANSPARENT SPINNER BASES  FIVE SECTORS

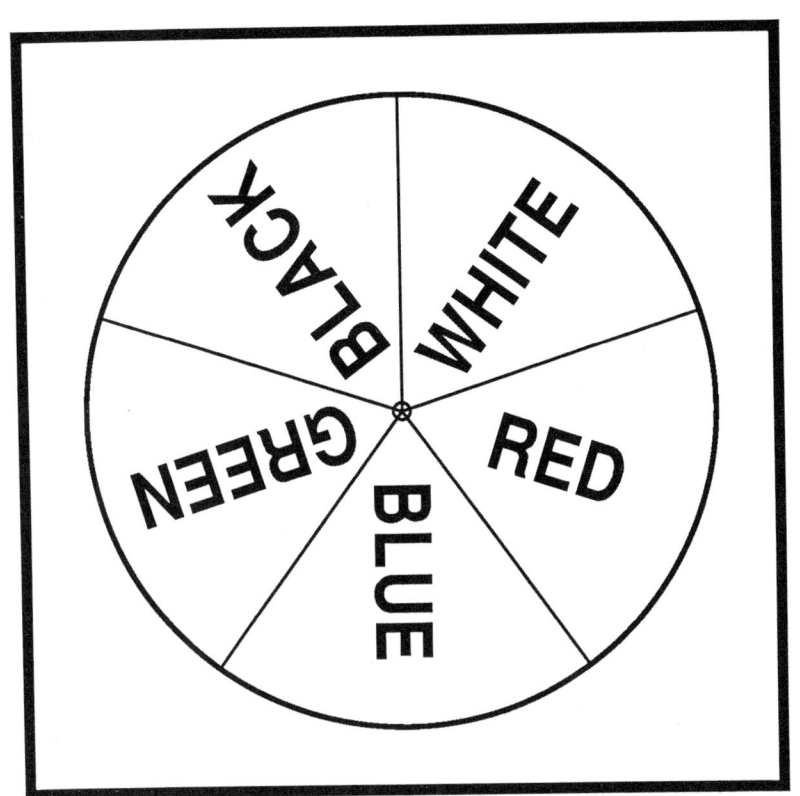

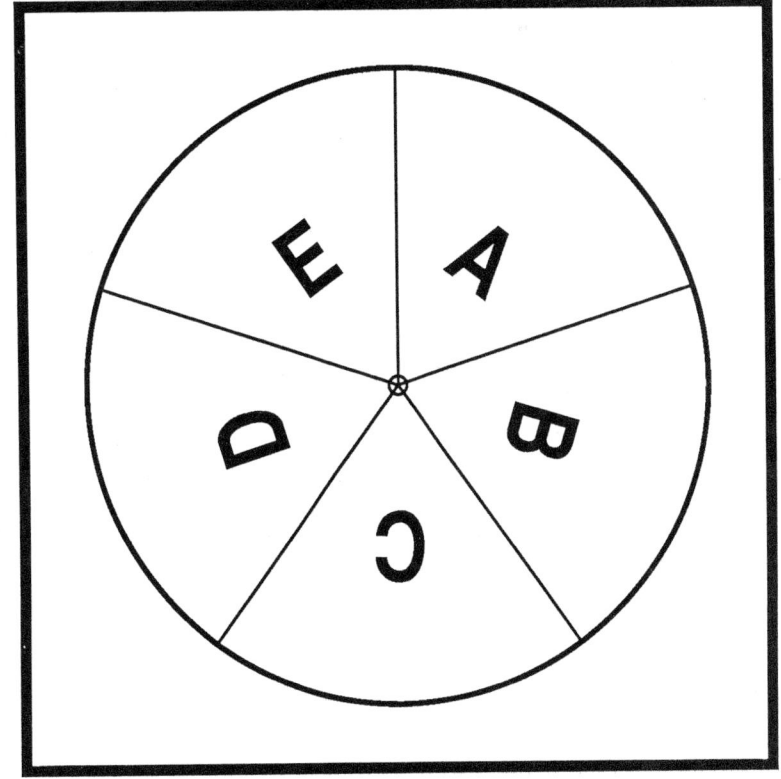

COPYRIGHT © 1987 BY DALE SEYMOUR PUBLICATIONS

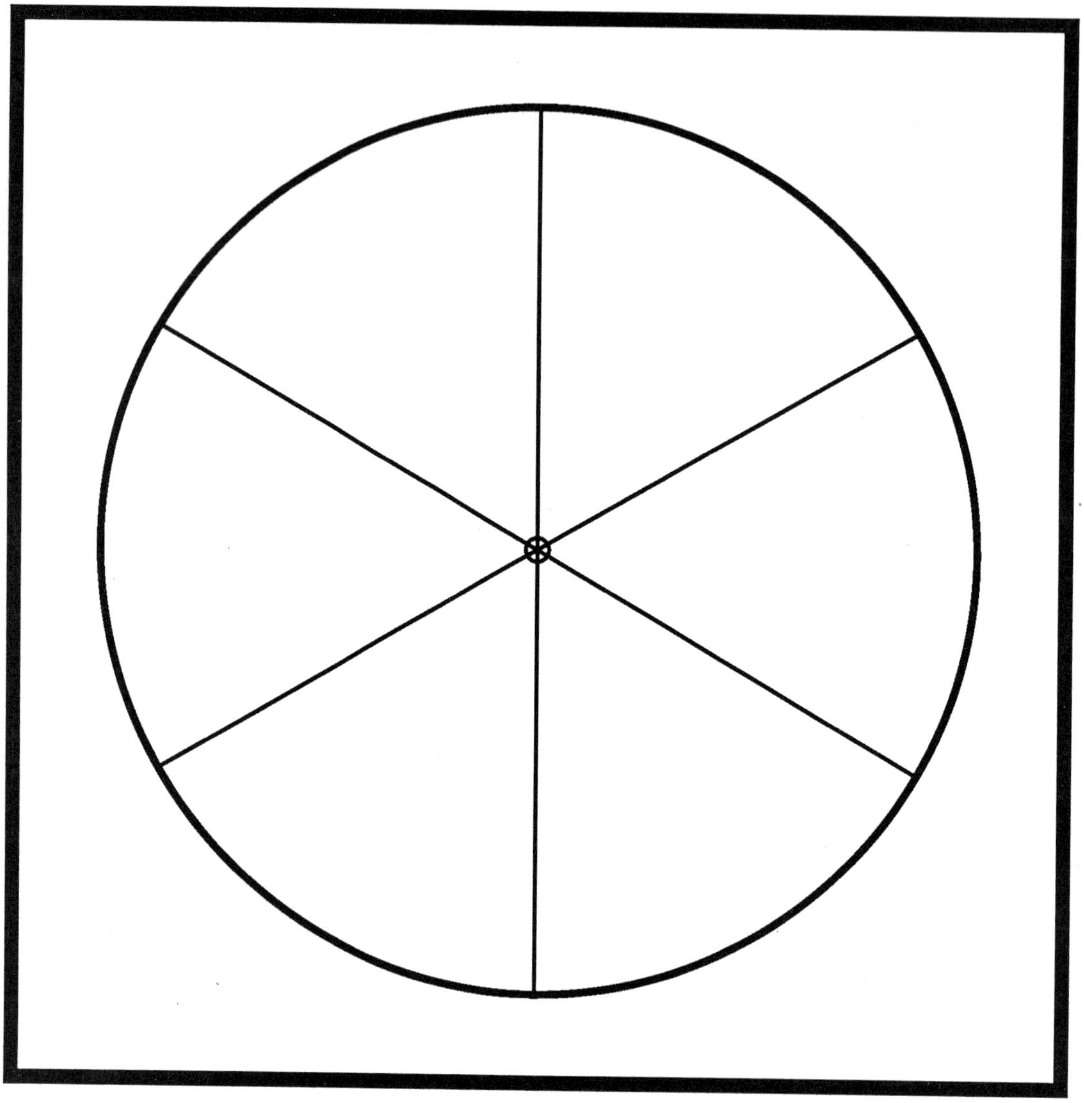

Transparent Spinner Bases  **Six Sectors**

Transparent Spinner Bases   SIX SECTORS

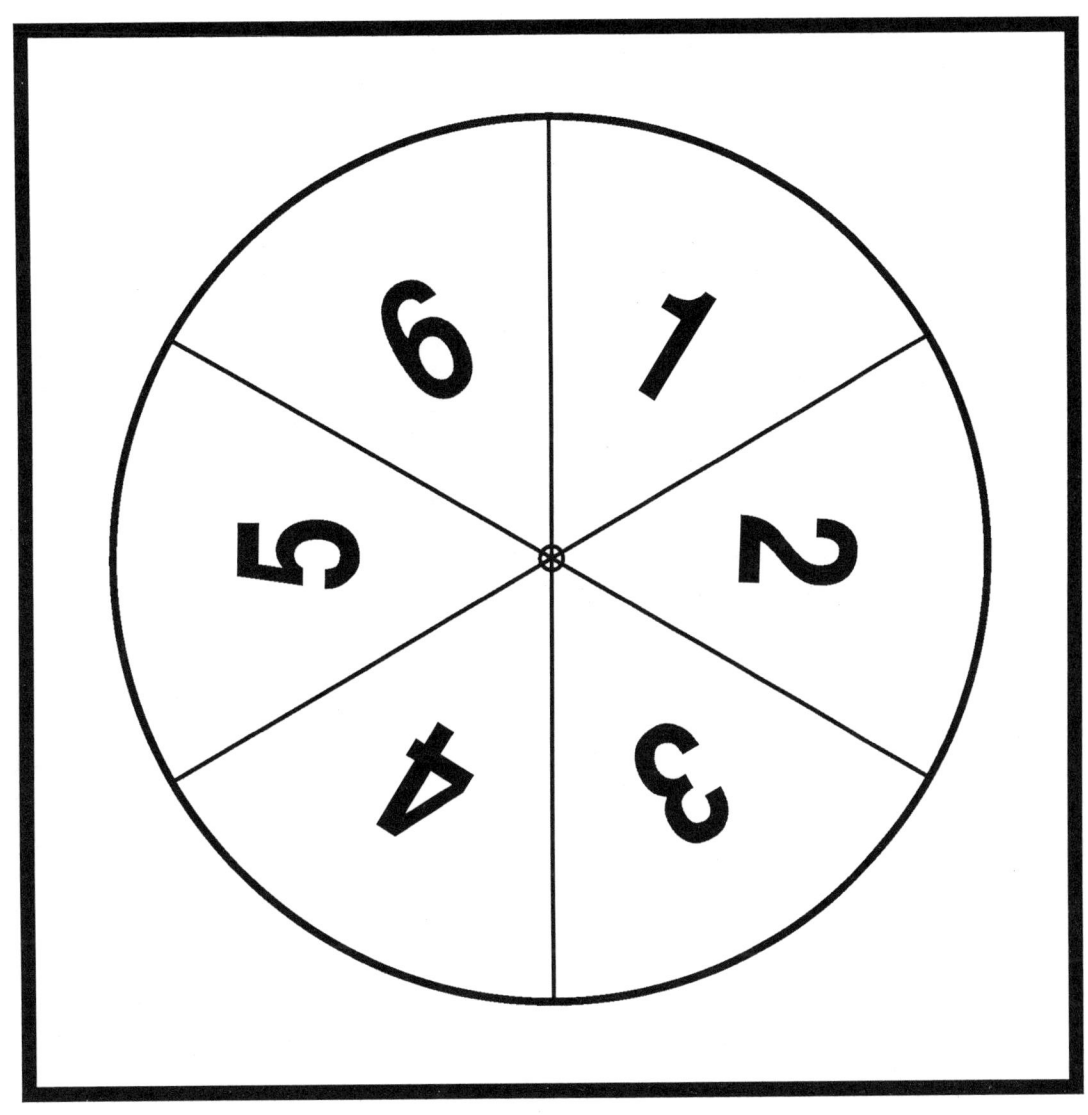

Transparent Spinner Bases  Six Sectors

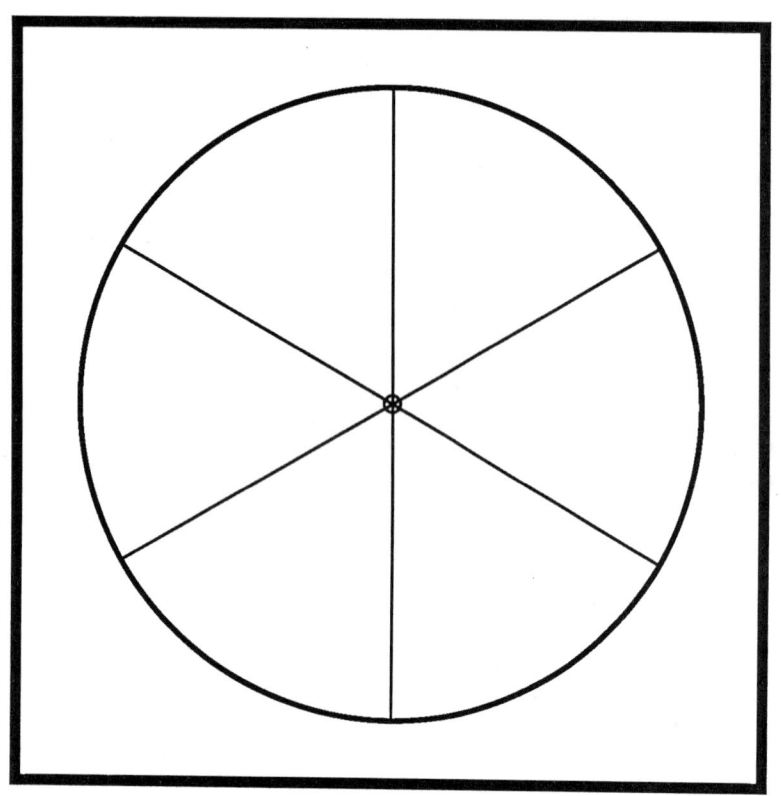

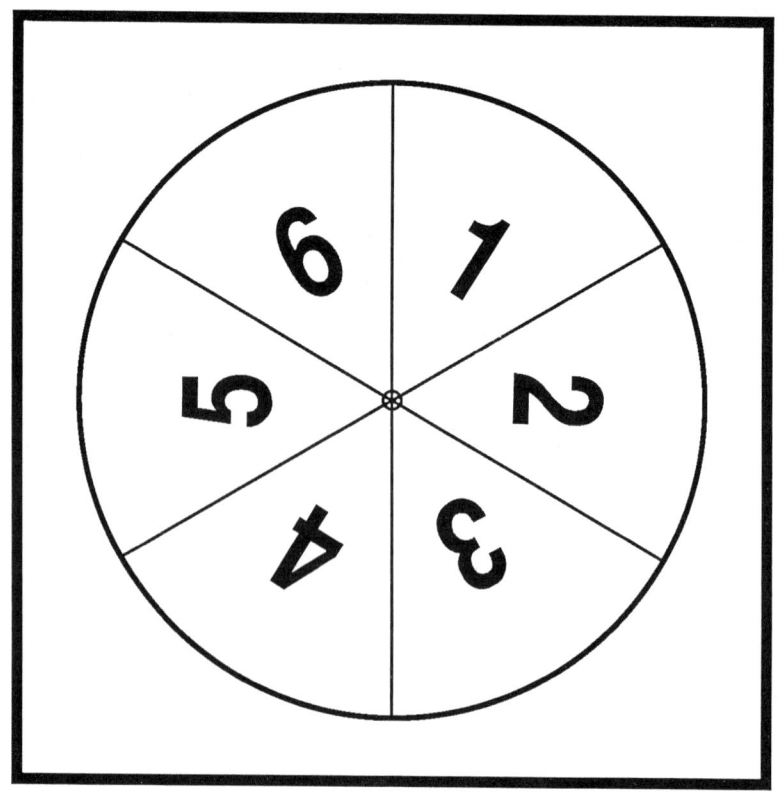

TRANSPARENT SPINNER BASES  DICE TOSS

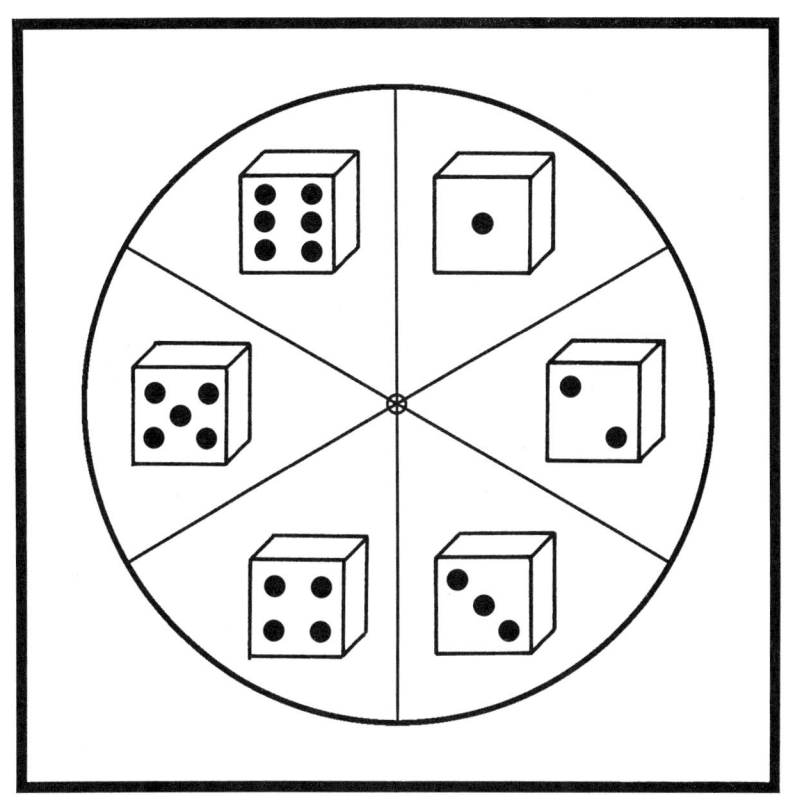

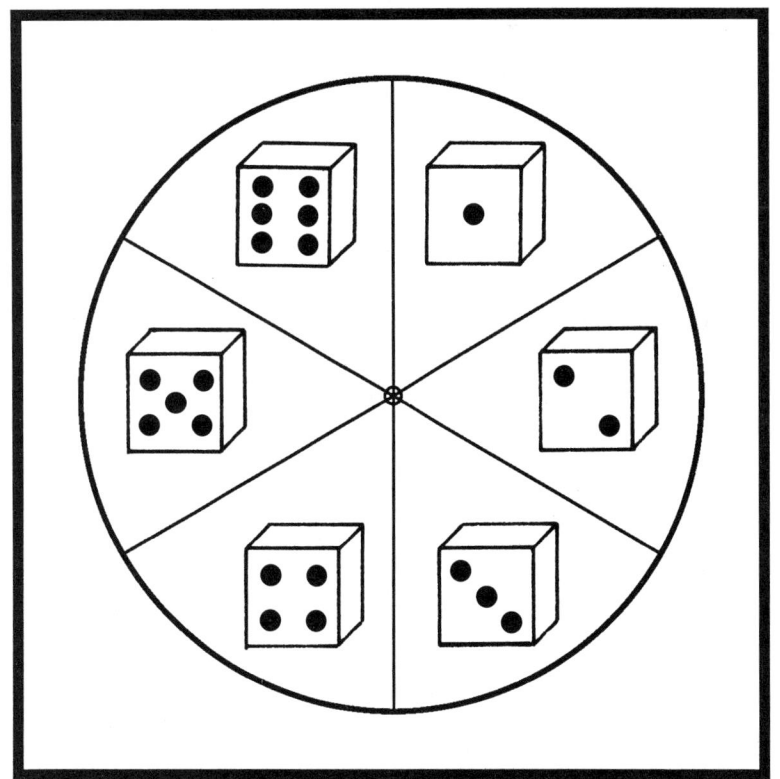

COPYRIGHT © 1987 BY DALE SEYMOUR PUBLICATIONS

Transparent Spinner Bases  Six Sectors

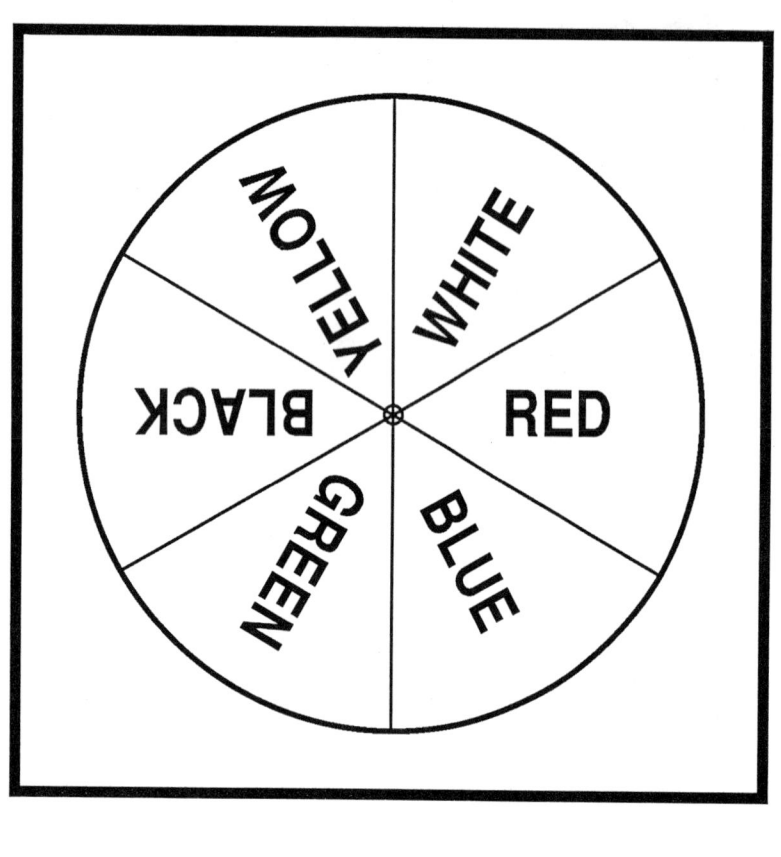

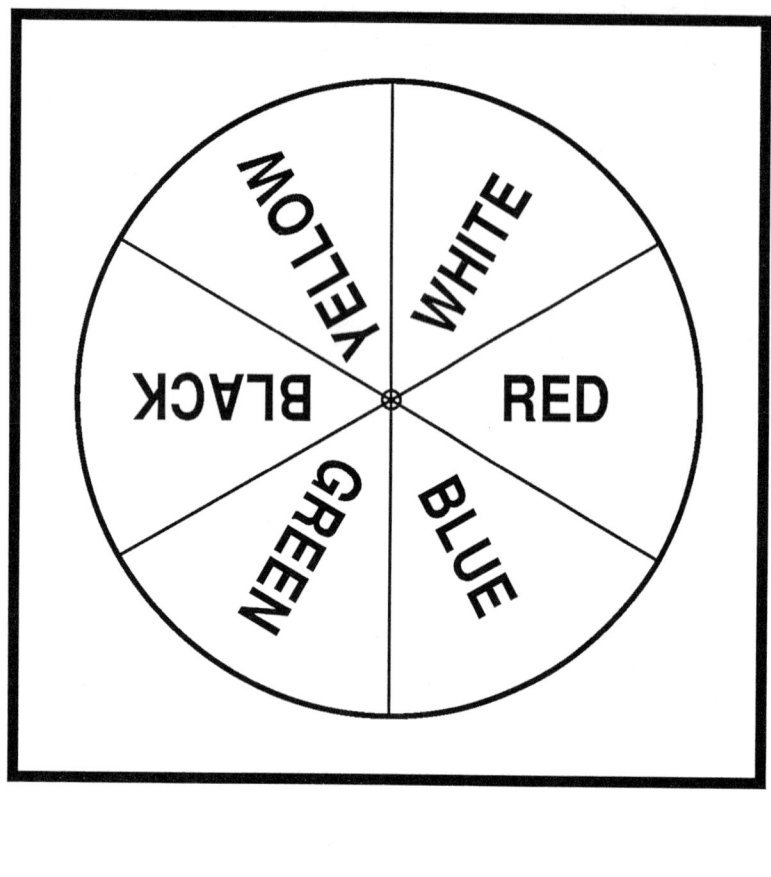

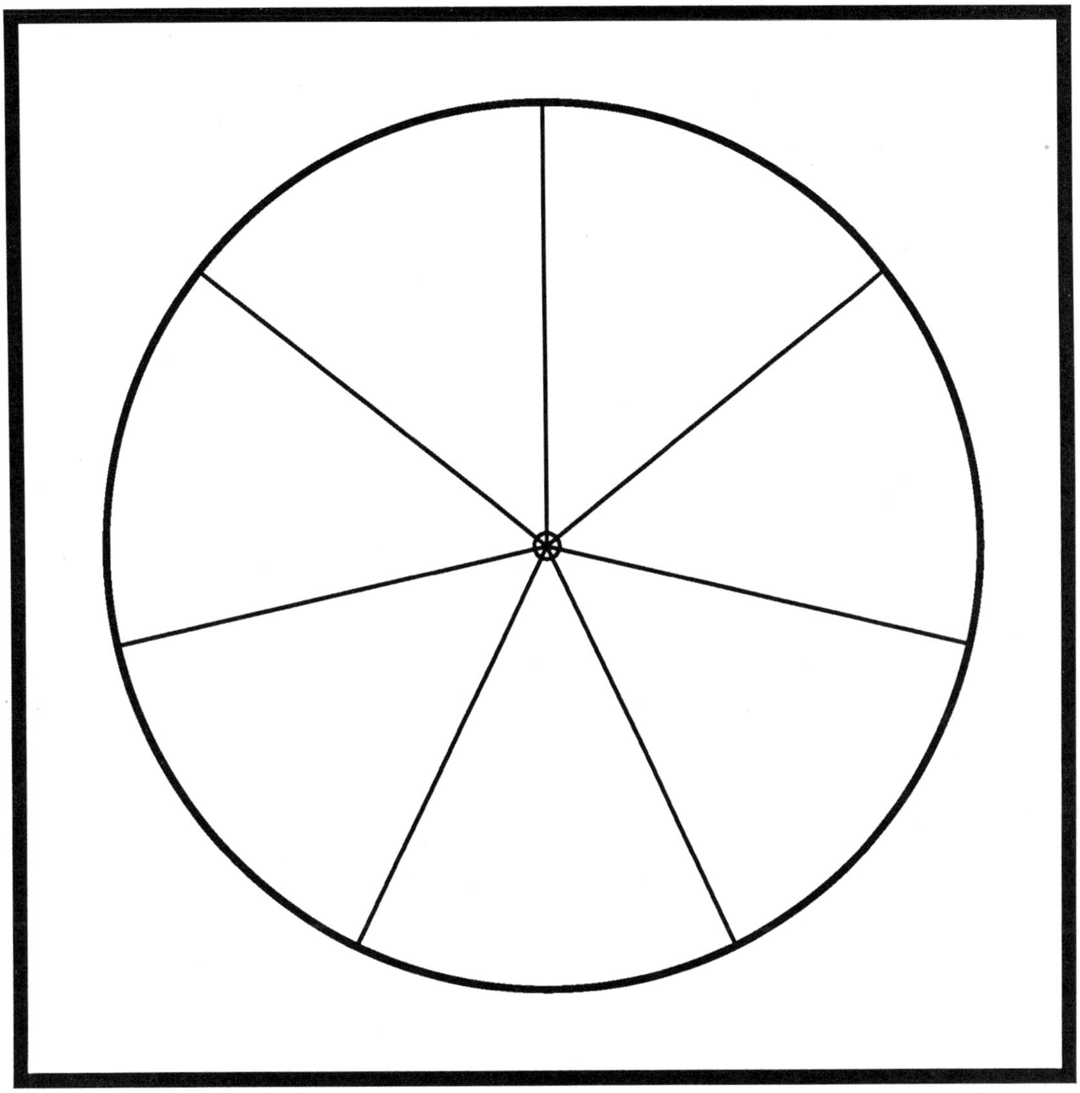

TRANSPARENT SPINNER BASES  SEVEN SECTORS

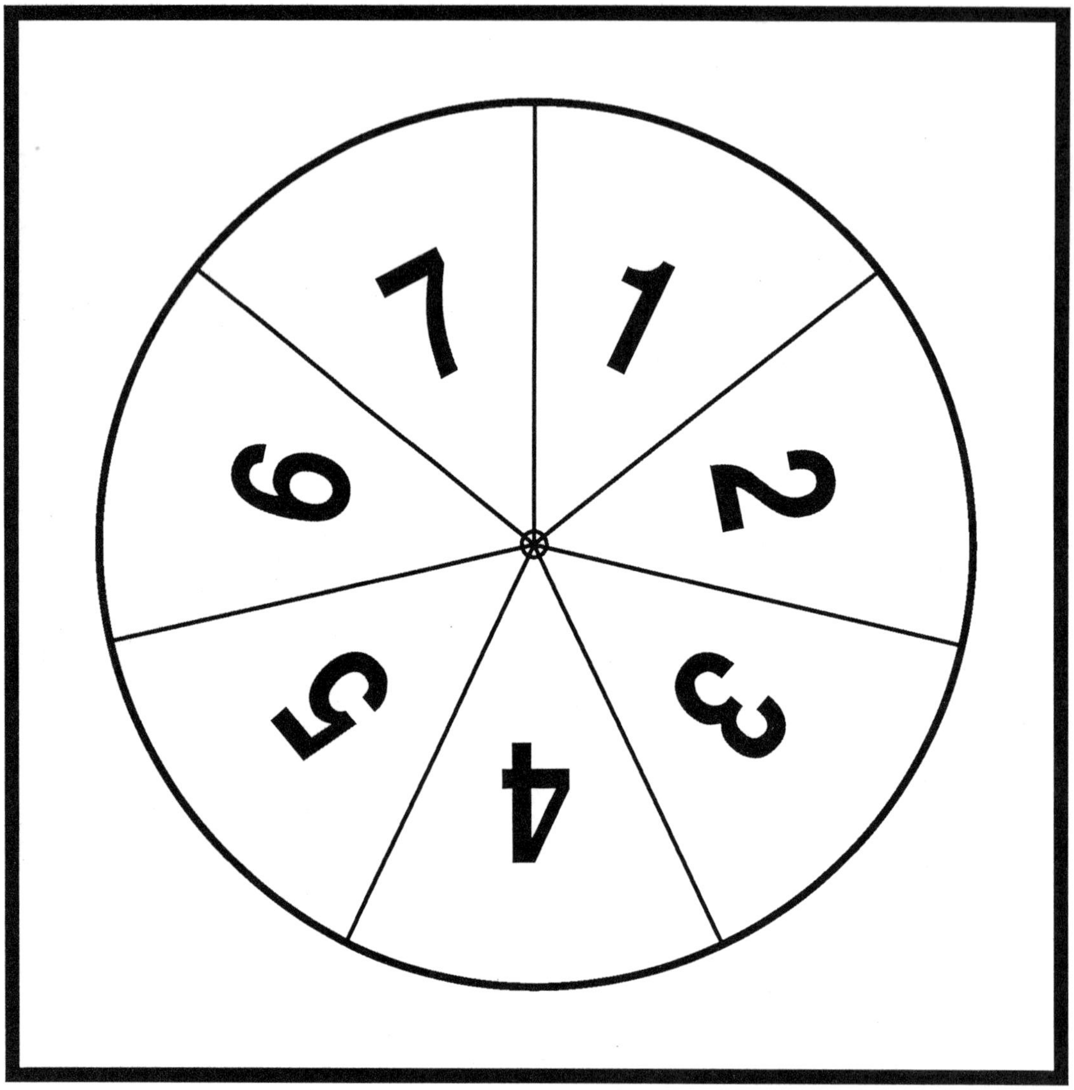

TRANSPARENT SPINNER BASES  SEVEN SECTORS

Transparent Spinner Bases  Seven Sectors

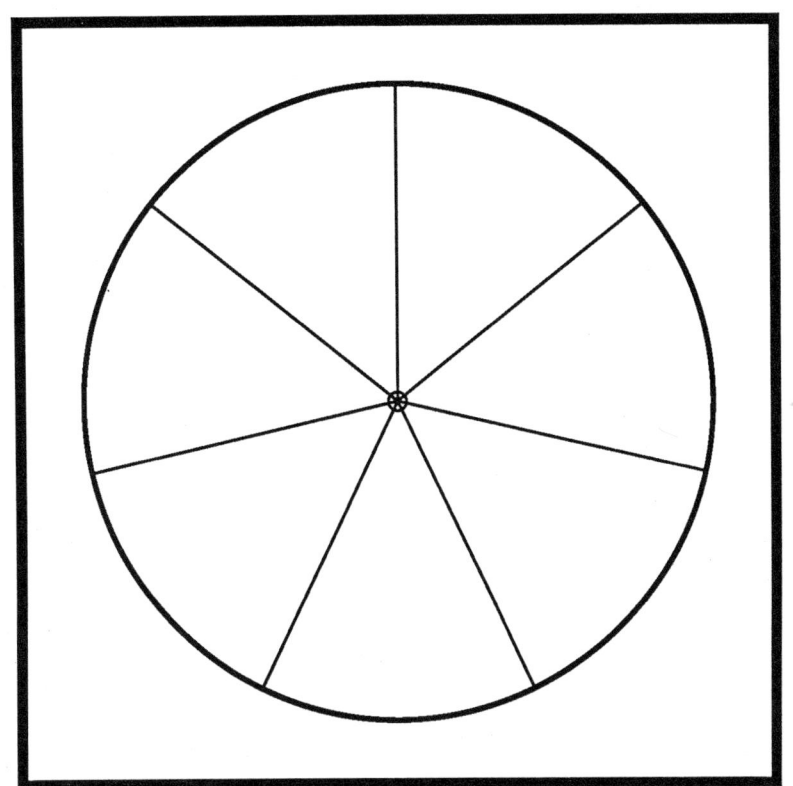

COPYRIGHT © 1987 BY DALE SEYMOUR PUBLICATIONS

TRANSPARENT SPINNER BASES  SEVEN SECTORS

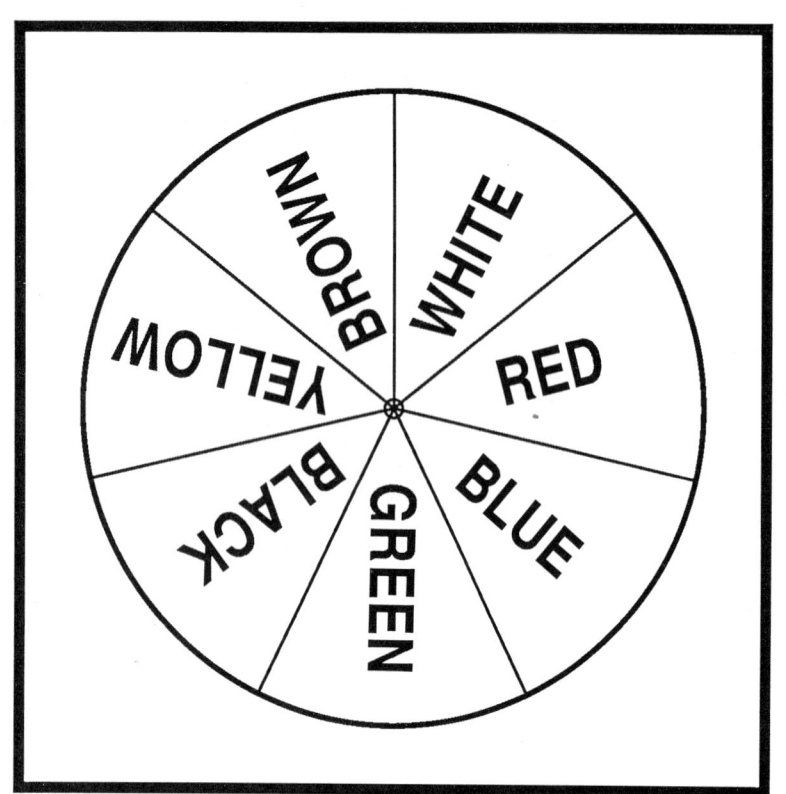

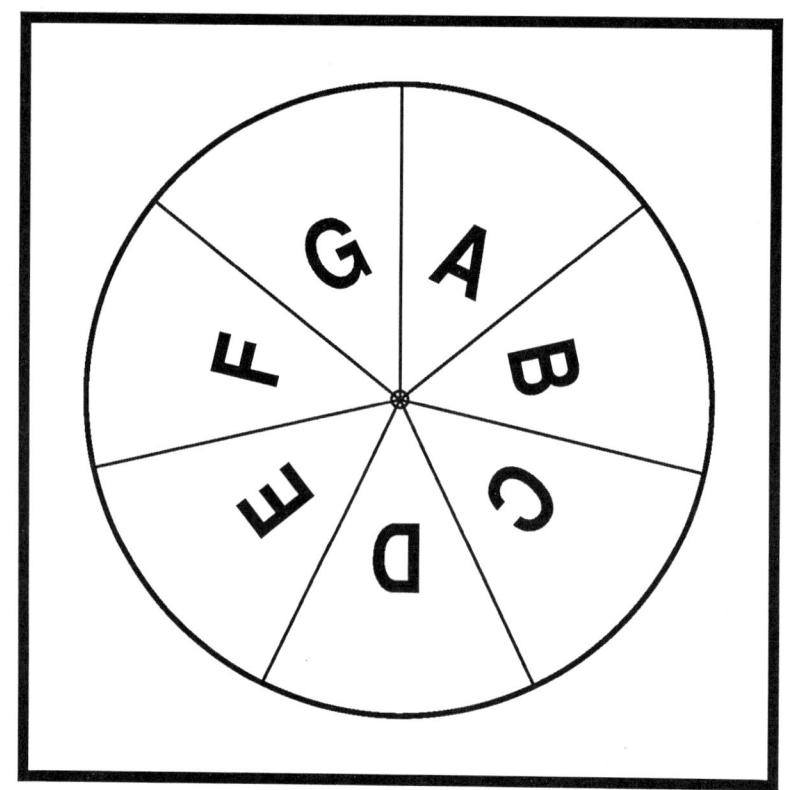

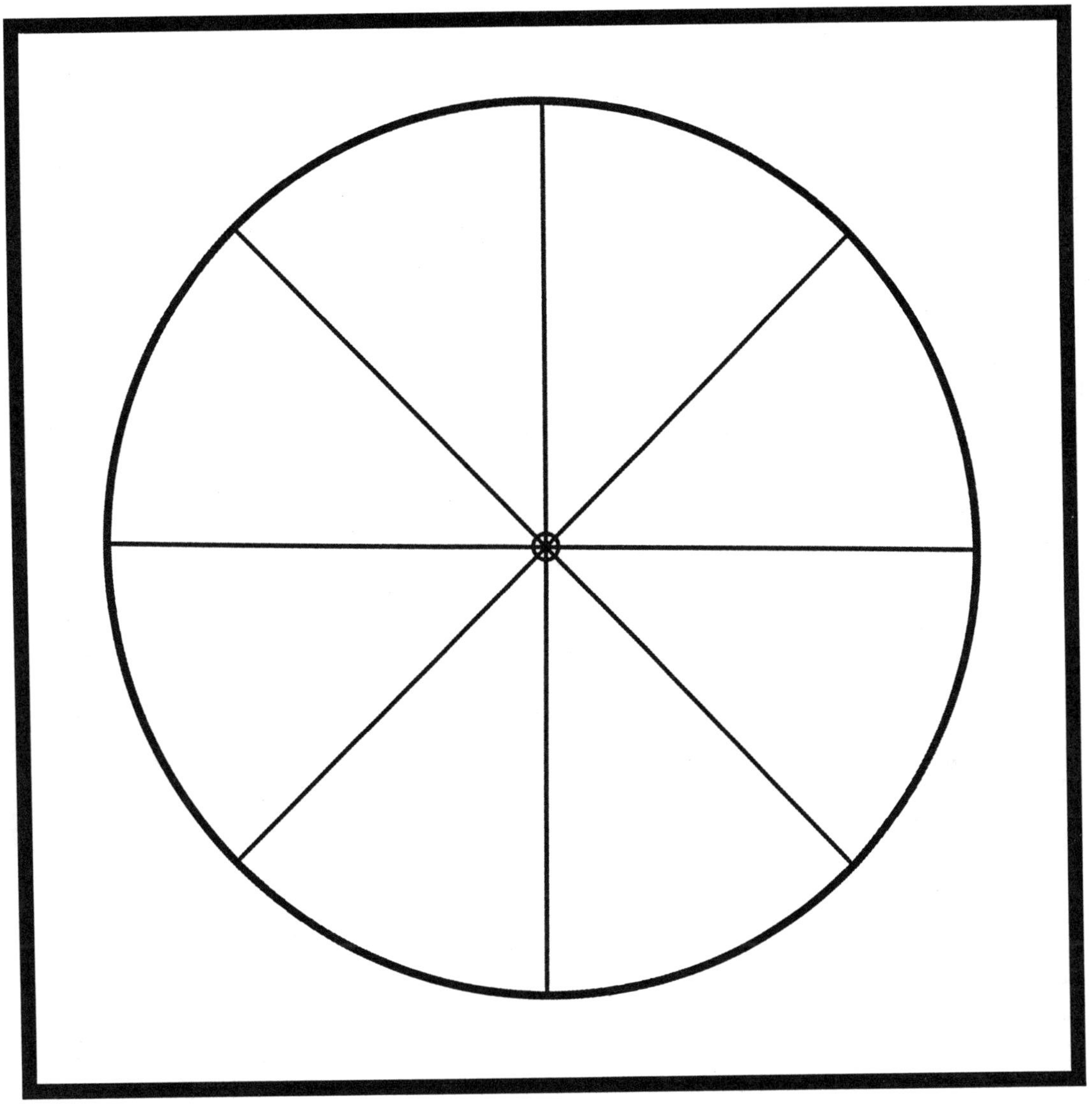

TRANSPARENT SPINNER BASES  EIGHT SECTORS

TRANSPARENT SPINNER BASES  EIGHT SECTORS

Transparent Spinner Bases  Eight Sectors

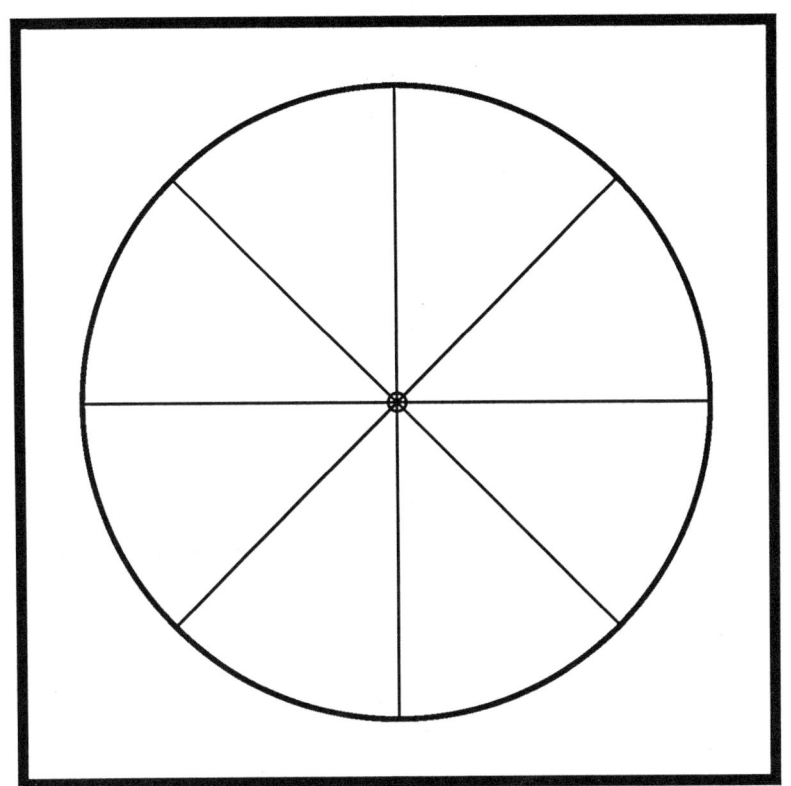

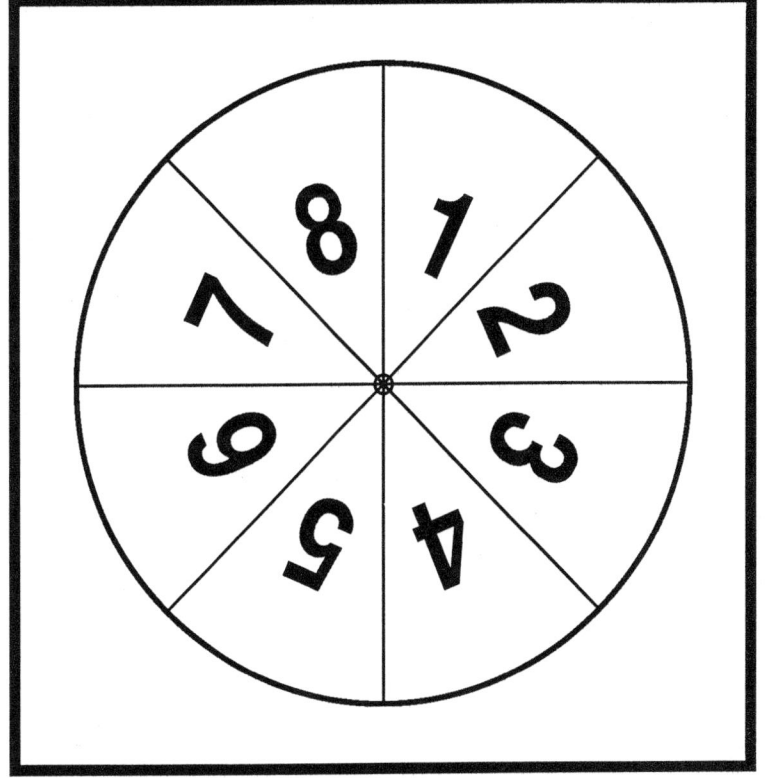

COPYRIGHT © 1987 BY DALE SEYMOUR PUBLICATIONS

Transparent Spinner Bases  Eight Sectors

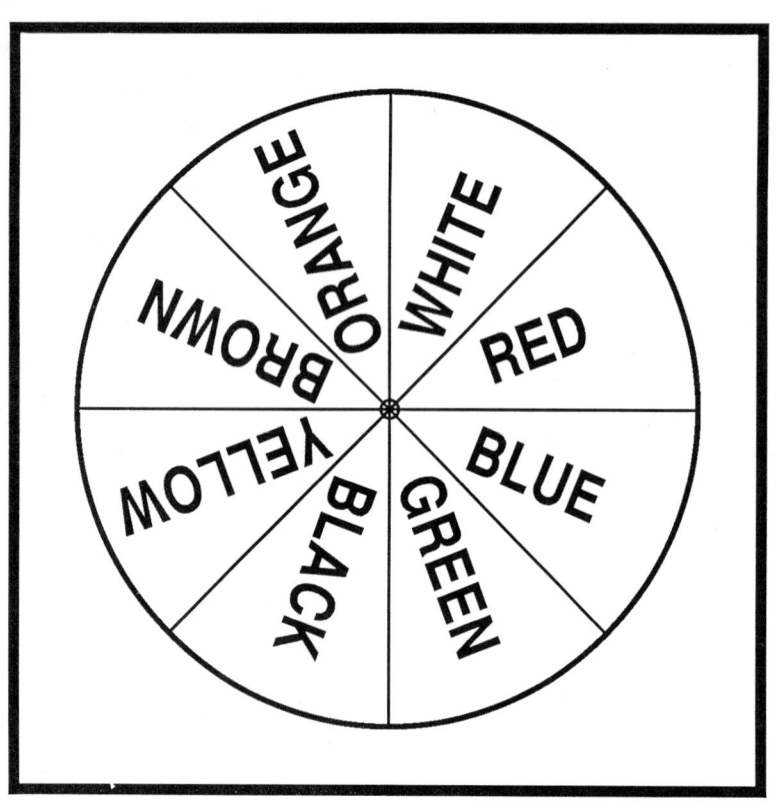

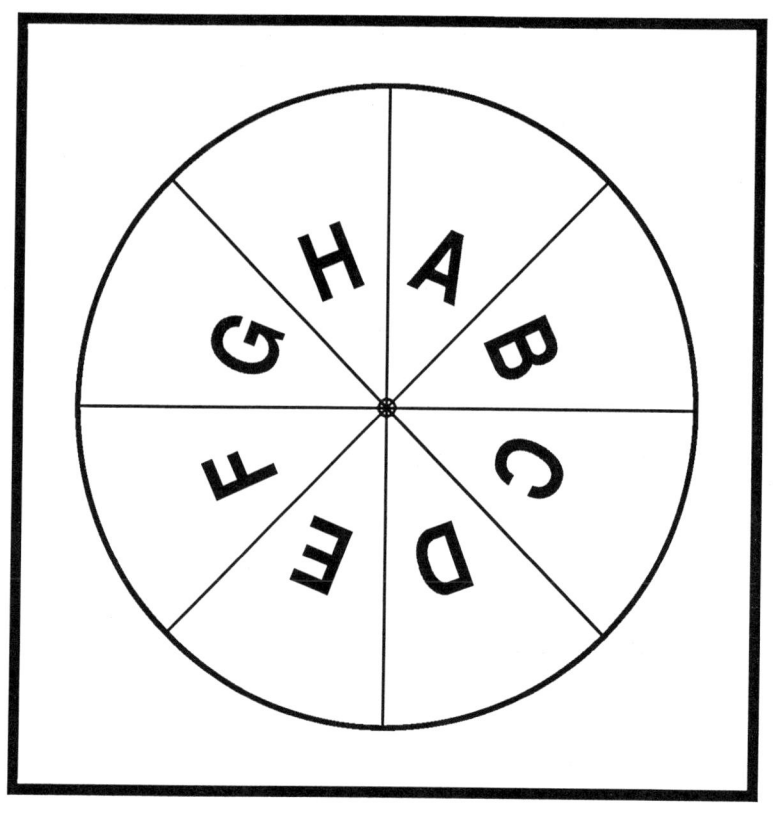

TRANSPARENT SPINNER BASES NINE SECTORS

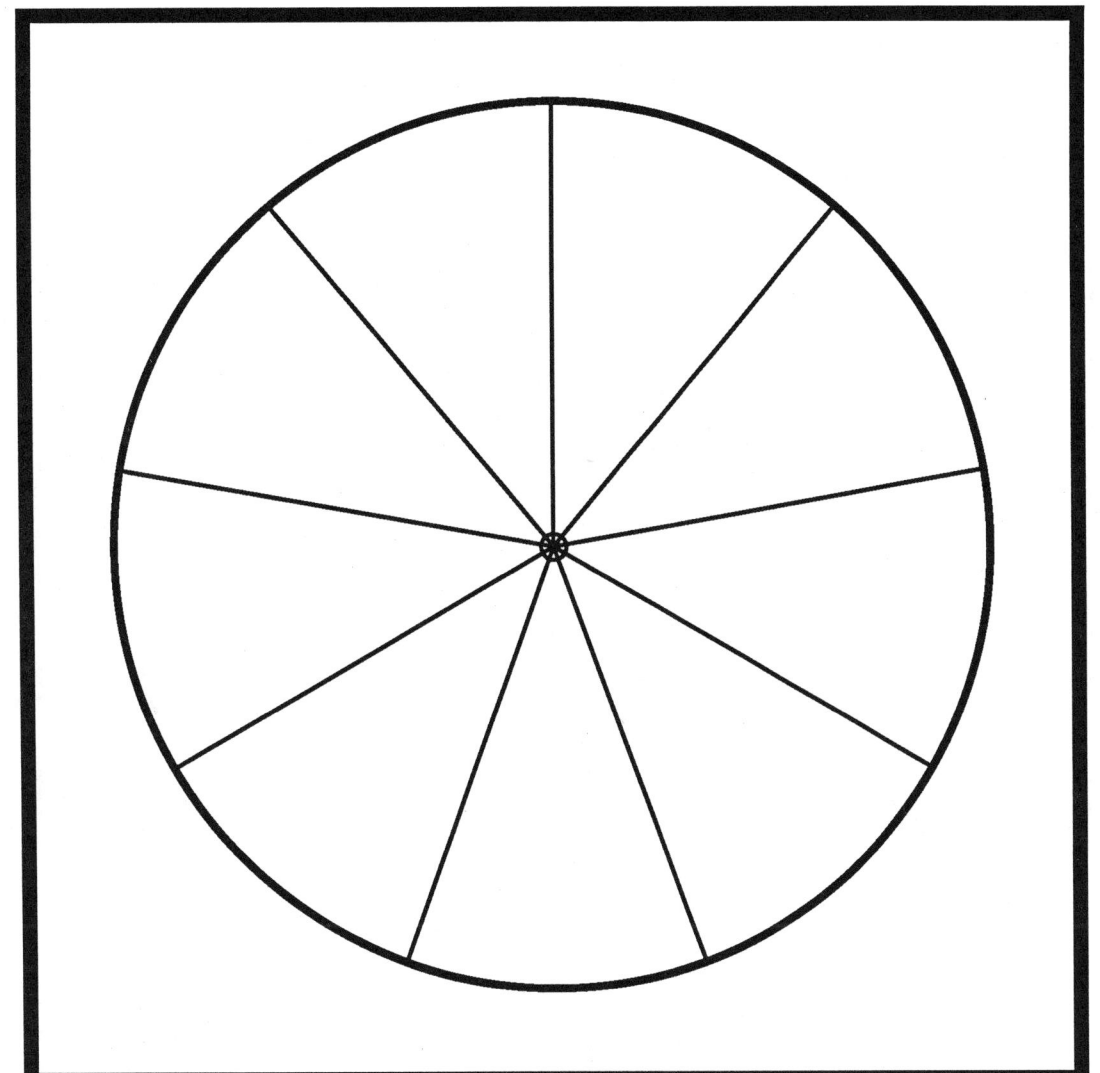

TRANSPARENT SPINNER BASES — NINE SECTORS

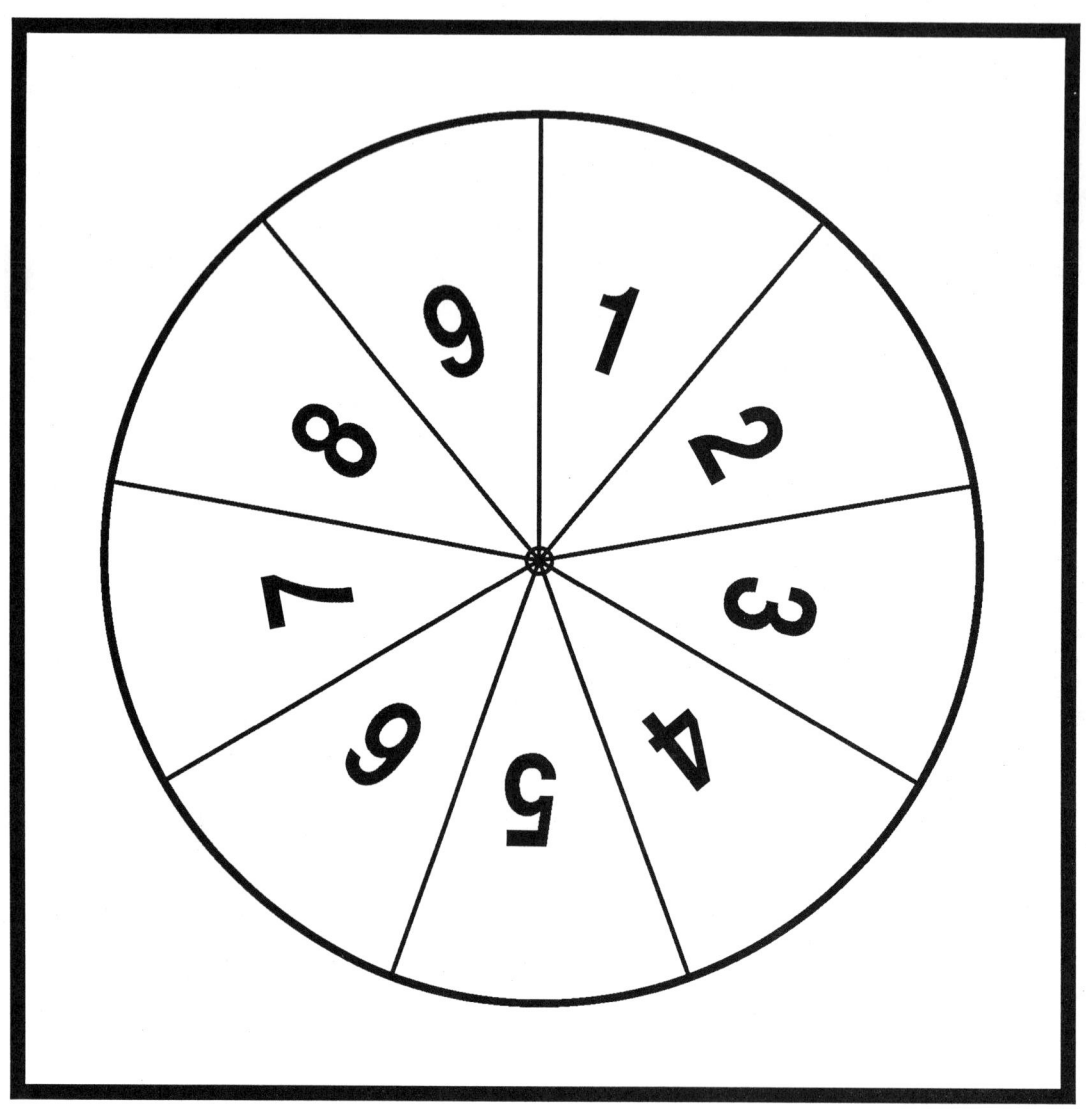

34 COPYRIGHT © 1987 BY DALE SEYMOUR PUBLICATIONS

Transparent Spinner Bases  Nine Sectors

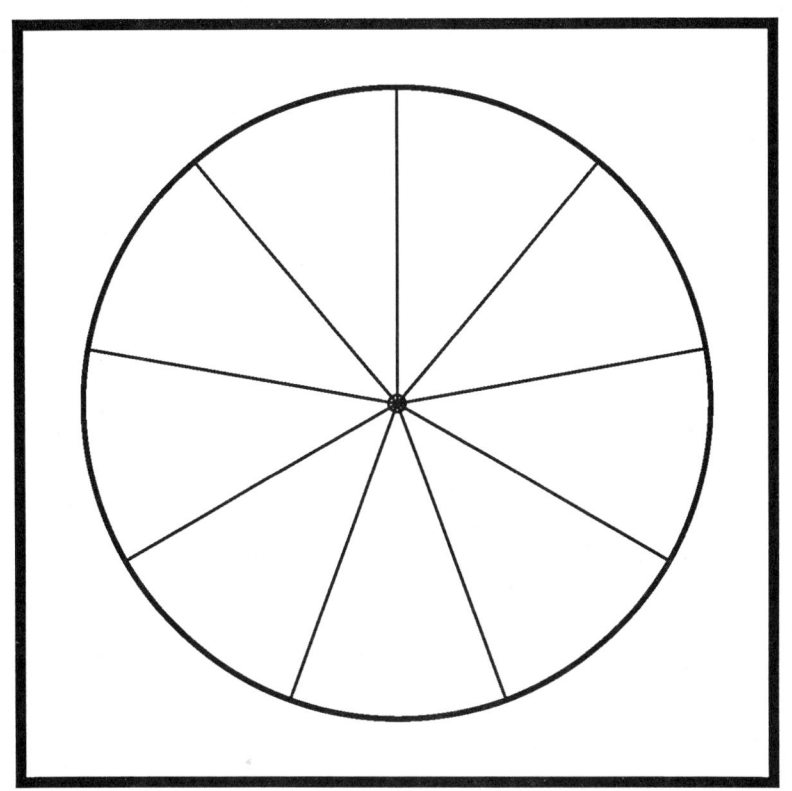

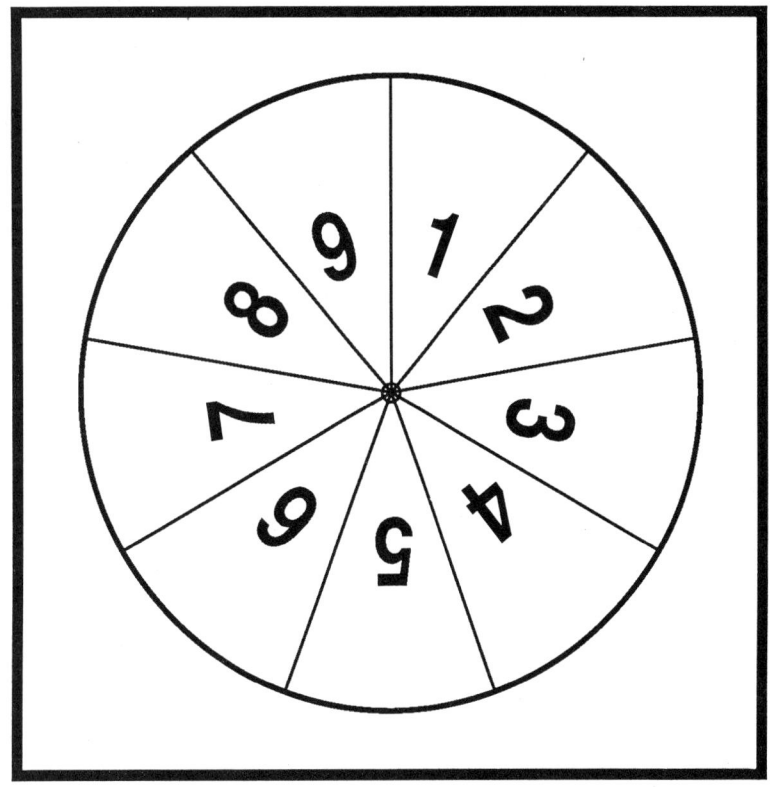

COPYRIGHT © 1987 BY DALE SEYMOUR PUBLICATIONS

Transparent Spinner Bases  **Nine Sectors**

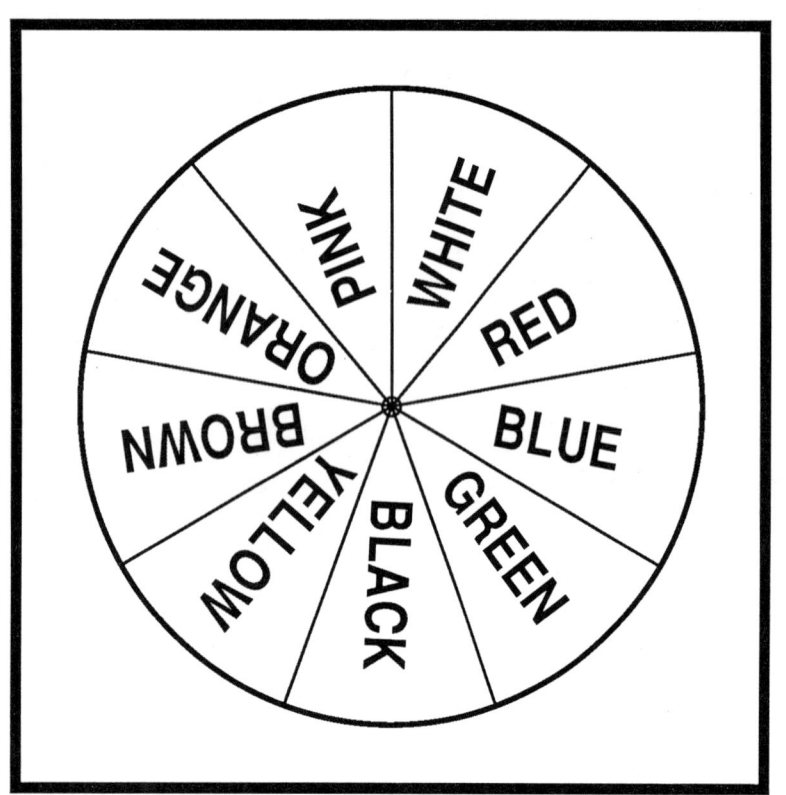

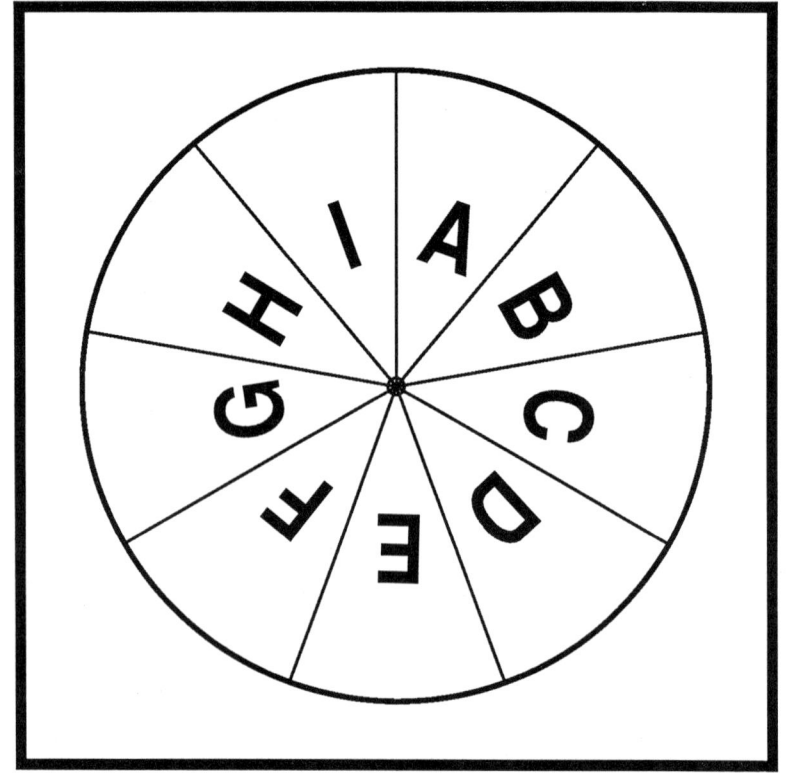

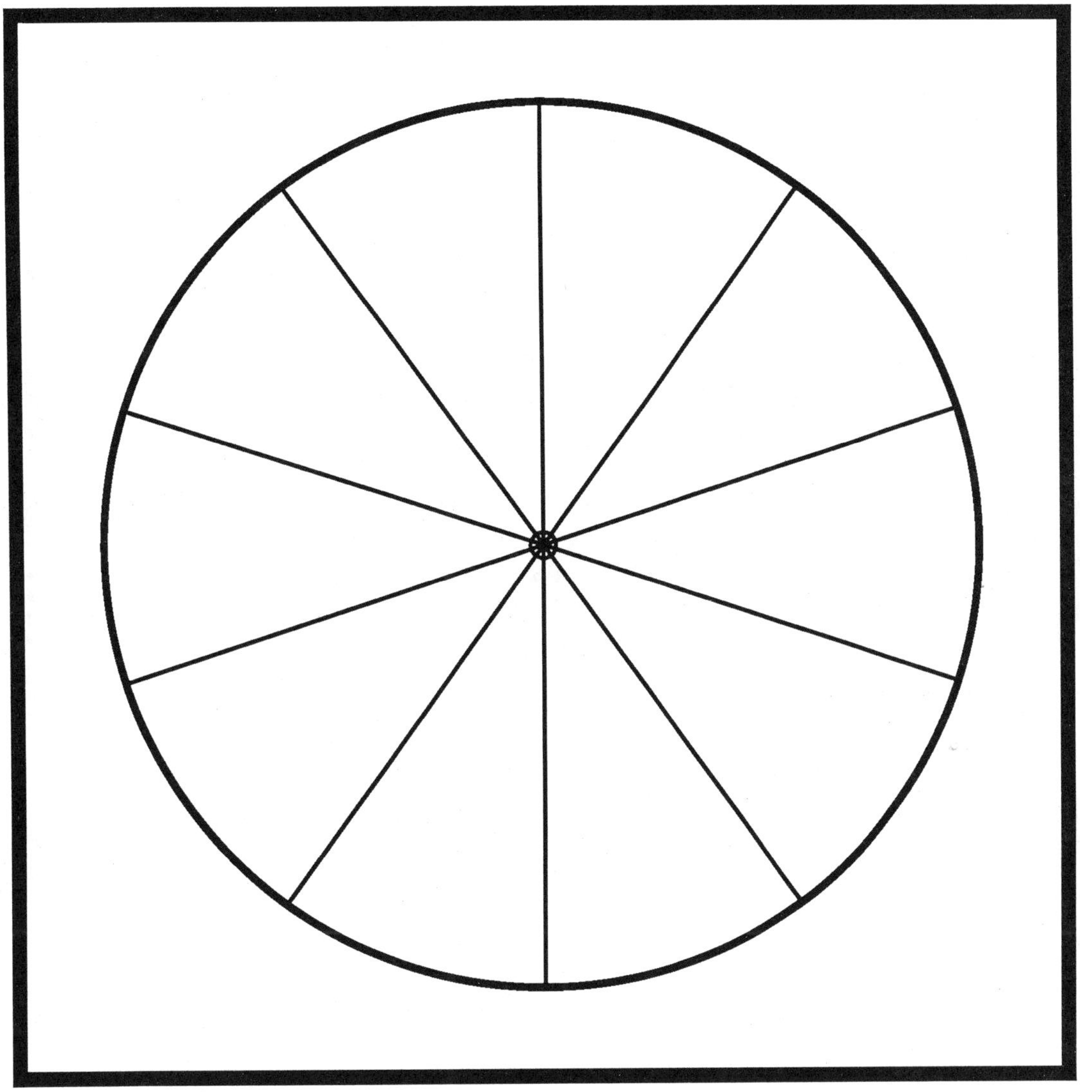

TRANSPARENT SPINNER BASES  TEN SECTORS

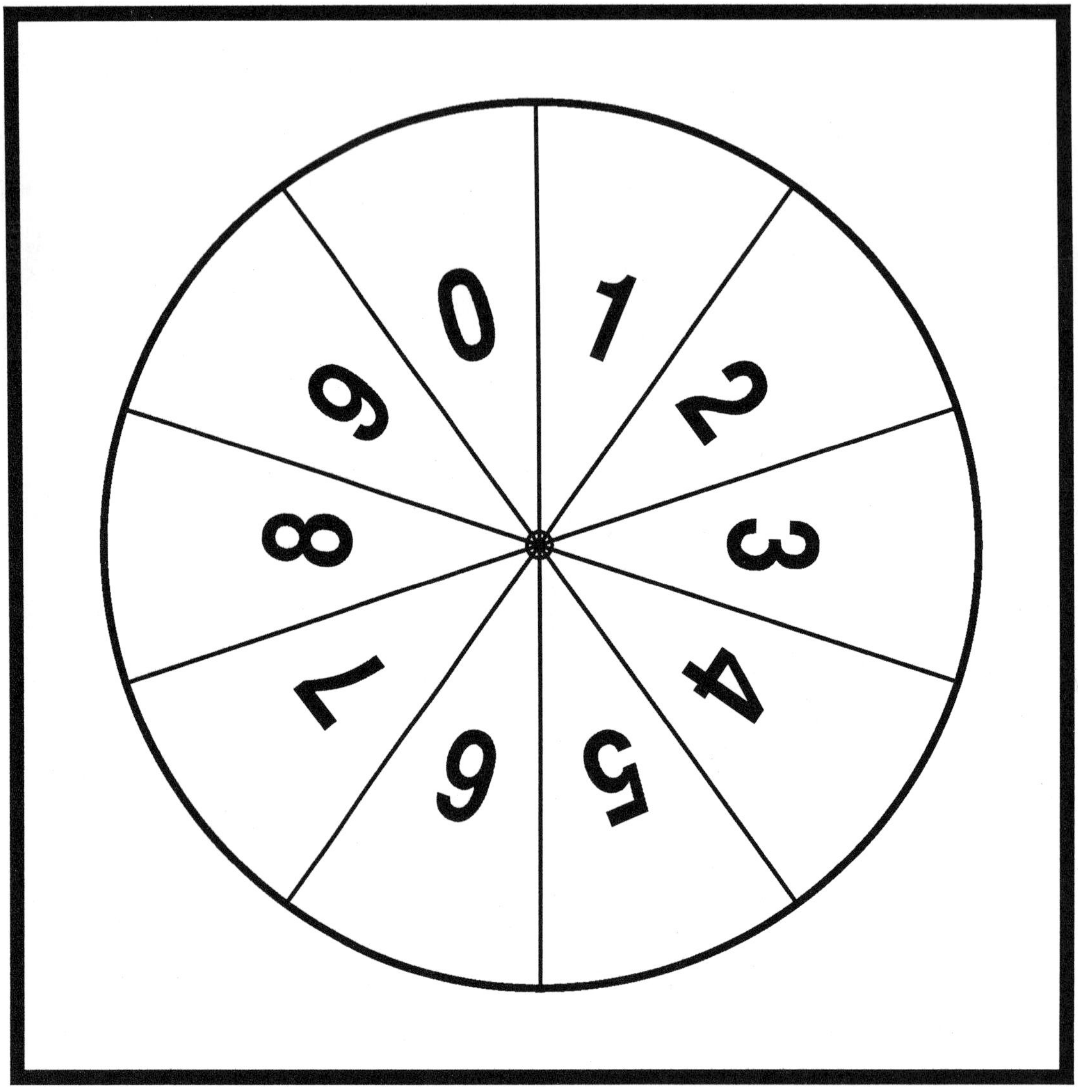

TRANSPARENT SPINNER BASES  TEN SECTORS

TRANSPARENT SPINNER BASES — TEN SECTORS

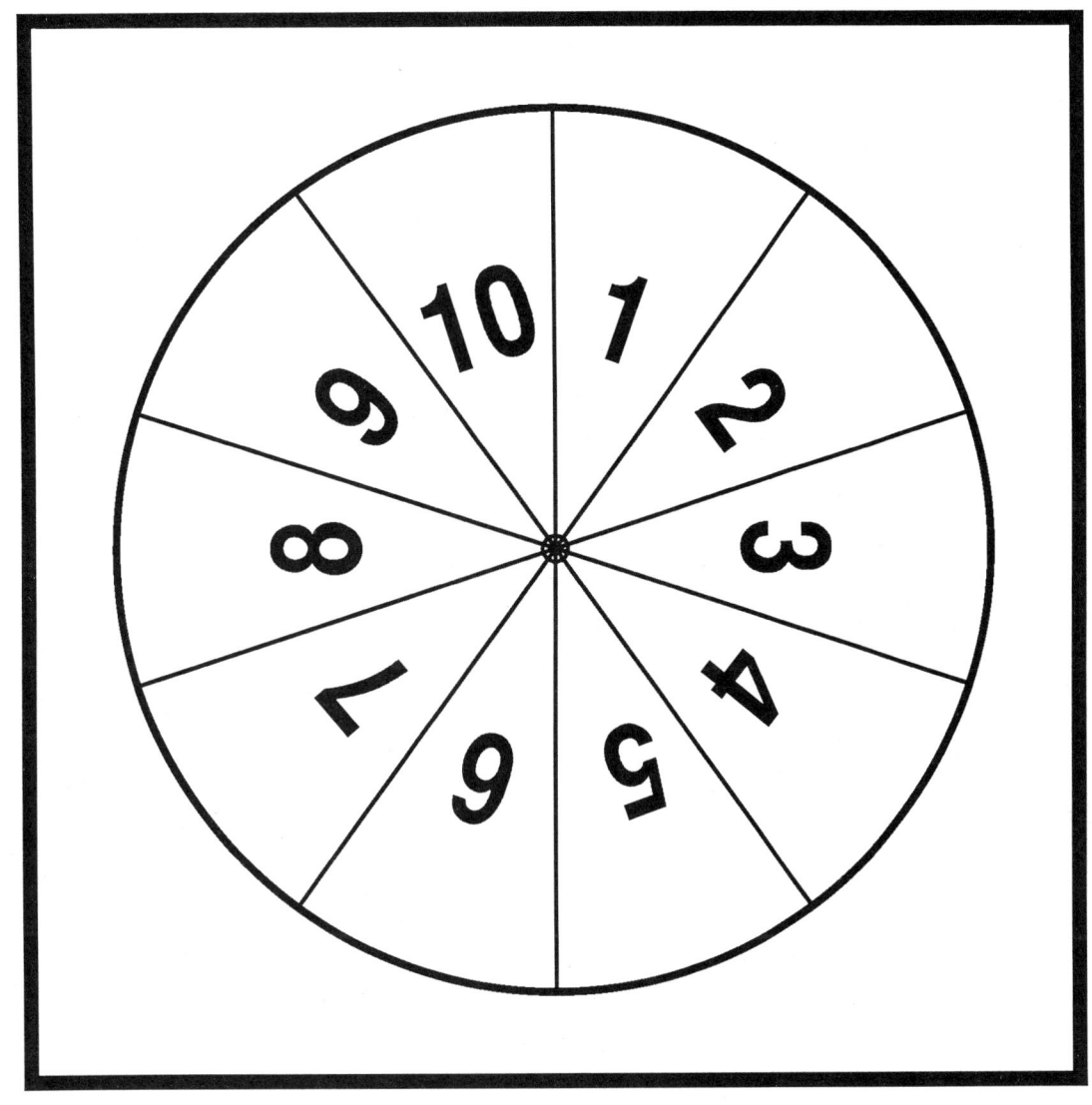

Transparent Spinner Bases  Ten Sectors

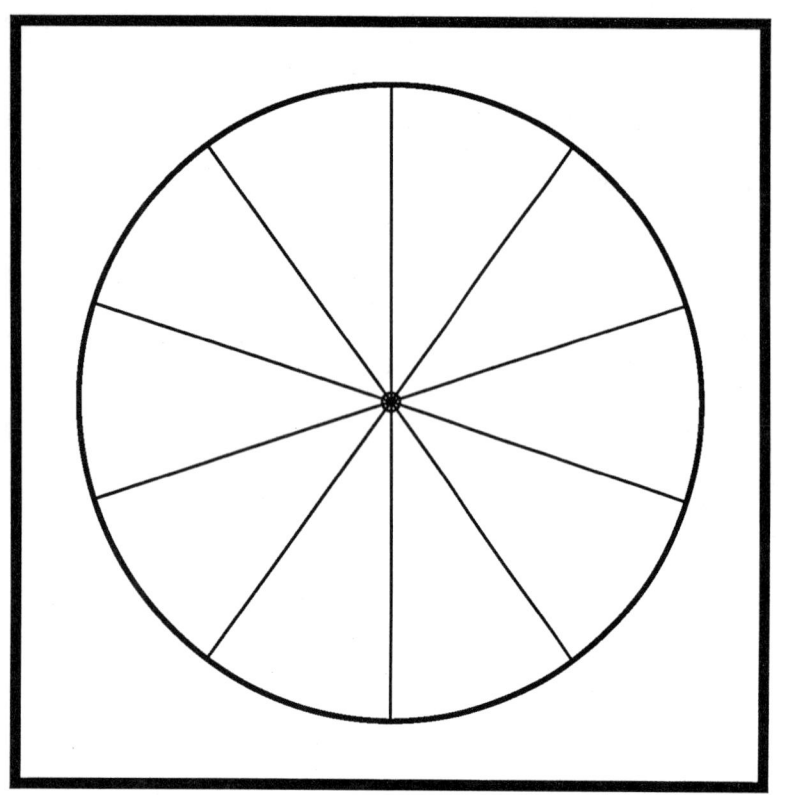

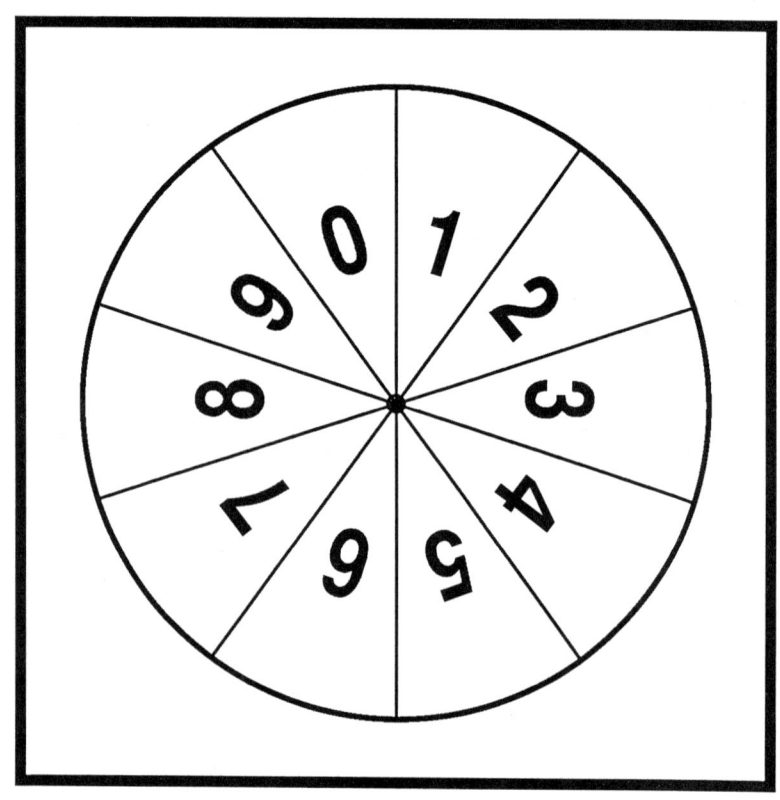

TRANSPARENT SPINNER BASES  TEN SECTORS

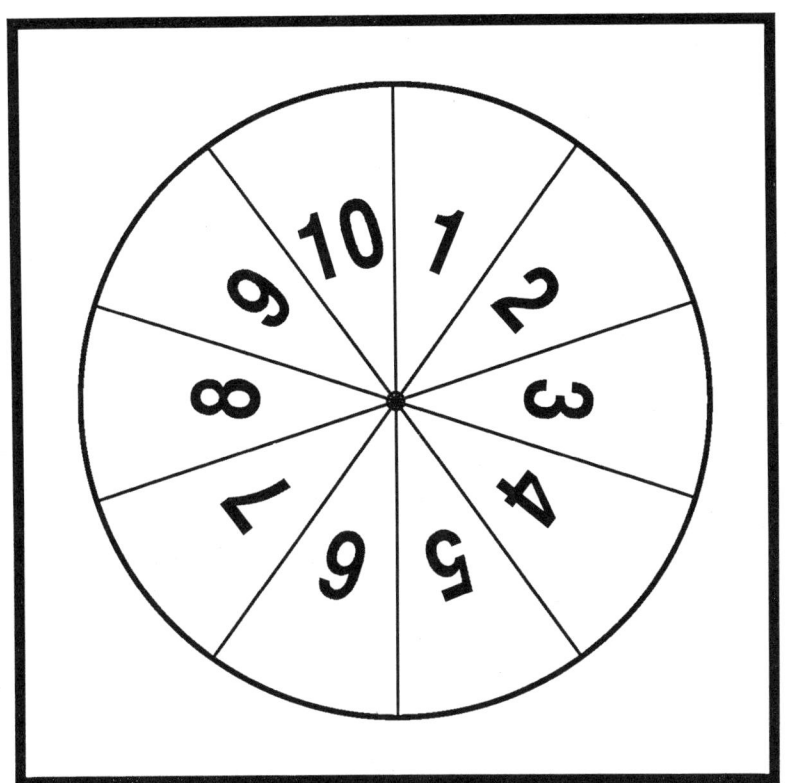

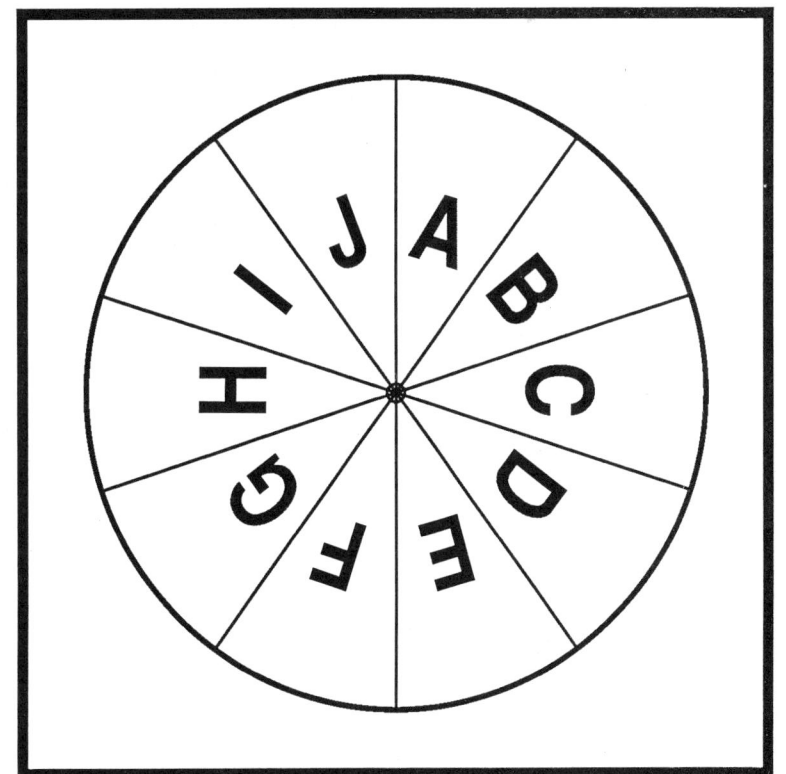

Circular Protractor

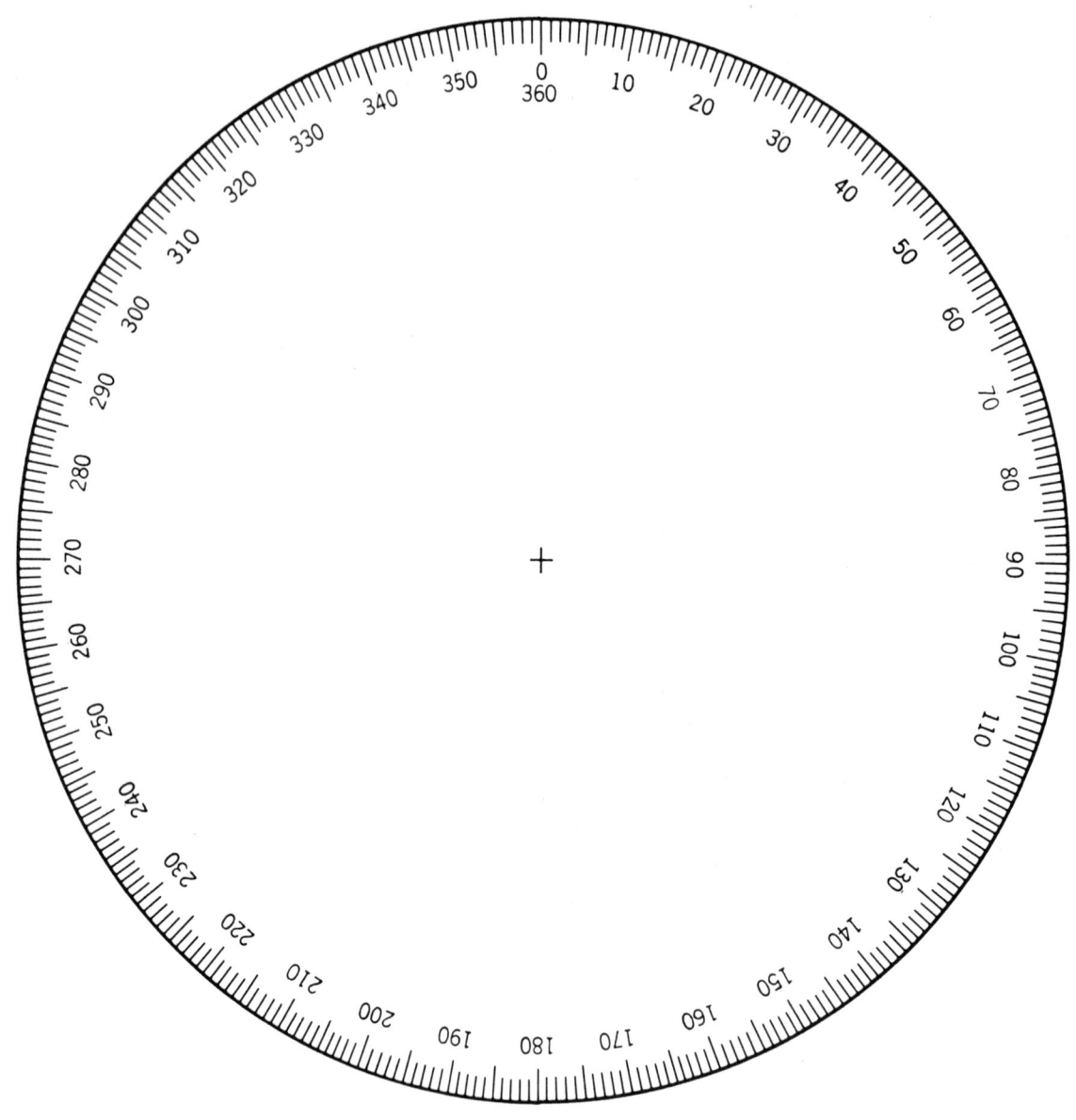